The Survival Guide to Journalism

The Survival Guide to Journalism

Dan Synge

The Survival Guide to Journalism

ISBN 13: 978-0-33-523785-2
ISBN 10: 0-33-523785-1

Published by:
McGraw-Hill Publishing Company
Shoppenhangers Road, Maidenhead, Berkshire, England, SL6 2QL
Telephone: 44 (0) 1628 502500
Fax: 44 (0) 1628 770224
Website: www.mcgraw-hill.co.uk

British Library Cataloguing in Publication Data
A catalogue record of this book is available from the British Library.

Printed in Great Britain by Bell and Bain Ltd, Glasgow.

The McGraw·Hill Companies

Contents

Acknowledgements

Sincere thanks to my star contributors Clare Gogerty, Paul Clarkson, Miranda McMinn, Sarah Cooper, Jane Cornwell, Simon Wright, Emily Benet and Mike Stanton. Many thanks also to Dan Adams (cover design) and Peter Lloyd (illustrations) for their inspired visualization of this book. I am indebted to my wife Miranda for her encouragement and support.

Introduction

Do journalists really need a survival guide: a manual to see them through the challenges of each working day? Admittedly, we're not talking about Arctic exploration, divorce or post-nuclear fall-out, but practically any profession that I have experienced requires some well-honed survival skills. Journalism is no exception.

Indeed, having worked in journalism for over a decade, I, like anyone else, have had to adapt over the years; social diary contributor, music reviewer, newspaper columnist, motoring editor, freelance feature and travel writer, editor of contract titles, antiques correspondent, illustrated book writer … it should be evident from my various journalistic guises so far that you rarely stand still in this profession.

This book, therefore, is aimed not only at students of journalism, but also anyone from any background who has seriously thought about making a living (full- or part-time) through their writing or editing skills.

Having read it, I hope that you will be able to apply some of the following journalistic principles straight away as well as take advantage of the up-to-date information on where the best opportunities are. My advice is deliberately hands-on and straight to the point, and is based on my direct experience of working for newspapers, magazines and online publications.

For added authenticity, I have included tips and testimonials from a range of top working professionals, all of whom, incidentally, are highly-adapted survivors.

In our exciting but often uncertain industry, it really does pay to have the right survival skills. There are exercises for you to try out, easy-to-follow checklists and short **Q&A** sessions (**Ask Dan**) to help clear up any uncertainties you may have about the subject of each chapter. Where possible, I have included useful links and contacts to organizations that specialize in helping aspiring journalists to survive through those difficult first months and years.

I have tried to sum up the state of the industry today whilst including practical guidelines on news and feature writing. We examine the ins and outs of freelance journalism and specialist areas such as reviewing, sub-editing and travel writing, plus some of the exciting opportunities created by new media.

I hope, at the very least, that *The Survival Guide to Journalism* inspires you to pick up your pen and notepad and find inspiring and important new things to write about. I also hope it serves as an essential desk-side reference book for many years to come.

1

So you want to be a journalist?

'Journalism itself is a talent. It makes you very judgmental, very quick-witted. You can perform in front of people and work punishing hours.'

Former Daily Mirror editor Piers Morgan

When I set out on a career in journalism back in 1994, the media landscape set out in front of me was a relatively simple one to chart.

There were local and national newspapers, most of which recorded healthy circulation figures that looked set in stone for years to come. Then, of course, there were magazines: consumer, contract or trade.

Most young journalists started off by working for a local newspaper or a trade weekly. Having done their training in this hands-on arena, the more talented ones would end up on Fleet Street: *The Times*, the *Guardian*, the *Daily Express*, *The Sun* and other esteemed titles.

Although some of these publications were, and still are, competing for the same readers, they had yet to contend with 24-hour news channels, text and online messaging, free sheets, podcasts, digital platforms or anything else that is loosely described as 'new media'.

The more traditional forms of media appear to be suffering something of a setback in the wake of these exciting new developments, and yet paradoxically, there appear also to be increased opportunities for journalists, provided that they are prepared to adopt new skills to survive in this highly dynamic and ultra-competitive environment.

So while fledgling reporters were once expected to learn shorthand and type double-spaced hard copy on sheets of A4, tomorrow's media stars are filing exclusive film clips or interviewing Hollywood A-listers via social networking or messaging service sites. As one national newspaper insider told me: 'We're no longer just a newspaper, we're a media organization.'

Like any professional group, journalists have always had to respond to social and technological changes. As ever, those who embrace change best will have the greatest chance of survival.

The essential qualities

Needless to say, you are talented and hard-working with superb social skills and a CV that will impress anyone sitting in an editor's chair.

However, if you lack any of the five essential qualities below, a career in journalism is unlikely to get beyond the preliminary stage.

1 Curious

Do you know or care what your neighbours get up to? What's that exciting new building development all about? Why have the letter boxes in your street been painted yellow? Why is there a police officer stationed outside the house up the road? A natural-born journalist always finds the answers to questions like these. Some even become front page stories.

2 Self-motivated

Unless you already have envy-inducing personal contacts in the media, making it in journalism requires enormous dedication and an ability to find and develop your own contacts and stories. You must also be disciplined enough to manage your own workload, which, as any self-employed person will tell you, is a job in itself.

3 Knowledgeable

You'll need an acute awareness of what's going on now and what is about to happen in the near future. Reading a lot (not just your favourite daily paper or news website) is essential and you should have a reasonable knowledge of practically everything that is covered by print and digital media, whether it's the names of newly appointed cabinet ministers or the latest trends in the property market.

4 Literate

Not all successful journalists are great writers, but a more than average command of English and a love of language will give you a healthy advantage in what is an increasingly oversubscribed profession. If your skills are not up to scratch, read and study the work of reputable journalists and writers (see the **Recommended reading** list on p. 145)

5 Numerate

This doesn't only apply to trend analysts and science reporters. *All* journalists deal in facts and figures and the best ones know how to use them to their story's advantage. Numeracy also comes in handy when claiming expenses or negotiating a fee. In the long run, letting someone else do the sums for you can leave you seriously out of pocket.

How journalists work

Journalists are almost unanimously interested in breaking new stories or helping to add to both the reputation and circulation of their publication, yet they work in increasingly diverse ways.

First, there are the many different types of editorial roles on offer, be it a local news reporter, national newspaper columnist, freelance travel writer, arts reviewer or website editor.

All these people have highly contrasting working hours, salary packages, levels of influence and job satisfaction, yet all are considered journalists.

Take into account also the unstoppable growth of media empires and the increasing amount of online content over the last few years, and you have another reason for the job's diversity. Journalists today don't just take notes, file their copy then move onto the next story. They are expected more and more to record sound and video clips, respond to readers' emails, write online blogs and possess many other skills associated with our technological age.

Gone for ever is the mythological **hack** with his long Fleet Street lunches and worn out shoes. The twenty-first-century journalist is a multi-tasking, laptop-wielding wordsmith with an active and inquisitive mind, a finger on the pulse and the nose for a good story.

Here are some of the most sought-after editorial positions in the profession:

Publisher

Anyone from a global media magnate to a work-from-home with their DIY online newsletter can claim to be publishers. Essentially they are the people who finance and manage the publication, paying special attention to sales and advertising revenue, on which every publication's success is founded.

Although they should have more than a passing interest in what goes into the publication, essentially they are in the business of money and are always on the look out for new ways to make it.

Editor

The role varies depending on the scale and importance of the publication, but most editors will oversee and decide on the publication's editorial content (including news stories, **features**, layout, cover design, **headlines** etc.).

They should have a clear vision of where their publication is going and head regular editorial meetings with staff to generate suitable content.

Where relevant, they should also develop a good working relationship with their publisher in the drive for increased sales and advertising revenue.

Clare Gogerty on magazine editing

Clare is editor of *Coast*, the magazine for 'living by the sea'.

What are your everyday duties?

My duties vary according to where we are in the production schedule. Around press day, it is heads down, processing pages, reading proofs and dealing with last-minute crises. During the rest of the month, I am thinking about three issues at once: the one that is about to go to press (proofs to be read, copy and layouts to be tweaked), the following one (copy to be edited, shoots to be discussed), and the one after that (planning and commissioning).

I try to deal with some tasks for each issue every day to keep things moving along. I also chair a variety of meetings including planning, ideas, production and picture meetings, and attend budget, managerial and human resources meetings.

In between, I attend to an enormous amount of emails, many from freelance writers pitching ideas and PRs trying to place products.

Every so often I venture out of the office either to cover a story or to attend a coastal event. It is important for me to be familiar with the British seaside and there is no better way to do this than by actually visiting it.

What are the challenges of being a magazine editor today?

The challenges for *Coast* are its small resources. We have to produce a luxury title with a staff of seven and a tiny budget.

It also means that we have to be constantly inventive and resourceful about funding features, searching for free images, writing stories in-house, and sourcing free locations for shoots. Having a team of seven also means that everyone must be firing on all cylinders all of the time. To keep everyone motivated and not exhausted I try to instil a spirit of enthusiasm and excitement. It can be easy to lose sight of why we all do this when time is short and you are staring into the maw of another press day.

Many magazines are beginning to recover from the slump caused during the recession. *Coast* has been largely immune from it and our sales have risen. However, I feel they could have risen more if readers had more pounds in their pockets. So that has been a challenge too.

What makes the perfect magazine story?

Unlike news stories whose prime purpose is to deliver facts, a magazine article should amuse, stimulate and inspire. This is achieved by a combination of well-written copy and breath-taking photography. A little bit of wit never goes amiss either. The most important thing is to avoid indulgent art direction and too much cleverness. The secret is to know your reader-ship and deliver what it wants.

What skills do you think are needed to survive in the magazine world?

Talent is an obvious prerequisite (and it always rises) but as there are so many talented people looking for work at the moment, an ability to work hard and often late is becoming essential. Those journalists who go that extra yard and deliver more than is expected are the ones that are recommissioned or are offered staff jobs.

On the other hand, those who deliver copy late, overlong and don't follow the brief are soon forgotten. All they do is annoy the commission-ing editor who has to wade through their copy, cutting and rewriting it. We all want clean copy that whistles straight through to subs.

What was your first break in journalism?
I was working as an editor in book publishing when a colleague left to take a job sub-editing on Tatler. Another sub-editor position came up there and she suggested I apply. I wanted to break into magazine publishing so leapt at the chance. And, despite my state school background, they took me on! Soon afterwards, the chief sub-editor left and I was promoted into that position.

What advice would you give to anyone starting out in this business?
Never underestimate personal contacts. It is becoming increasingly tough to break into journalism, so you need to network as much as possible. Keep in touch with everyone you met at journalism school: they are the commissioning editors of the future. Join organizations such as Women in Journalism and attend industry events. If your face is known, you have a much better chance of getting work. If commissions are not forthcoming, then blog or Twitter. It is important to get your name out there.

When pitching for a story or a position, make sure you know the title thoroughly and apply to a person directly (i.e. take the trouble to find out names and positions of relevant editors). This sounds blindingly obvious but is repeatedly ignored. Grovel and flatter and say that it is your dream to contribute to the title.

Deputy editor

Working alongside the editor, the deputy has a rather more hands-on role and will work with budgets, commission articles and edit copy as well as cover for the editor's absence (editors are frequently 'in meetings').

They will have a firm grip on what has been planned for future issues and will also understand and advise on production issues such as page design and picture sourcing.

Paul Clarkson on being a deputy editor

Paul works for *The Irish Sun* and has a senior editorial role in both its Irish and Northern Irish editions.

What are your everyday duties and responsibilities?

Along with the editor, I have overall responsibility for all editorial content and management of staff and casuals in the paper. I also have control of all budgets in the paper, having assumed the managing editor role.

I also handle all dealings with the Press Ombudsman and liaise directly with advertising and marketing departments on a daily basis.

What ingredients, in your opinion, make the perfect news story?

The best stories don't need to be sensationalized – because they are just so astonishing. The perfect news story is something extraordinary happening to an ordinary person. And for it to be perfect you need the perfect photograph to accompany it and the perfect headline. If you can't get a perfect headline it isn't the perfect story.

How do you and your team go about finding stories? Are there any 'tried and trusted' methods?
My news desk has some staple sources to fill the holes: government and PR press releases, freelance agencies from Ireland and beyond, radio news etc. However, we demand exclusives from every reporter. They all have sources in various fields. On breaking events we *always* send a reporter. You never know what you will get from knocking on a door.

What skills are needed to survive in newspapers today?
It is all about being multi-skilled today. The industry is ever more competitive and the onus is on fewer people with more skills.

It is not just enough for a sub to be able to sub copy. More and more they will have to have design skills too. The same goes for reporters. They need a breadth of expert fields and be able to write on most subjects. It is all about speed, accuracy and a creative spark.

What was your first break in journalism?
My first break was blagging a job with music magazine *Mixmag* in Ibiza. I had no qualifications or experience, but loads of ideas and good copy. In newspapers, you need a minimum of a Postgraduate Diploma in Journalism to start you off. It can be easy enough to get a

sniff in newspapers through work experience, but make sure you make the most of it.

I got a placement with the *Daily Express* in London and I basically made myself a pest. I came in seven days a week for 14 hours a day and was eventually offered a place on their trainee scheme. In the event, I had already started doing shifts with the *Irish Daily Mirror* and they offered me a staff job back in Ireland.

What advice would you give to someone hoping to get into newspapers today?

The standard of graduates from journalism courses is sometimes very poor. The good candidates are good in spite of and not because of their studies. So forget the attitude and forget about trying to save the world through your cutting social commentary.

If you want to succeed you must be creative, have an innate sense for a good story. You must be intelligent and sharp to make you stand out from the crowd. Always be humble and willing to learn. Be thick-skinned. Be absolutely dedicated and be in it for the love of journalism and not the glory. The most successful people always take risks and make mistakes but never make the same one again.

Features editor

Feature stories (as opposed to news stories) are the longer, more human interest articles found in magazines and newspaper supplements, and these are normally commissioned and edited by a features editor.

Along with the editor, they chair regular features meetings in order to generate content while looking out for new, talented writers to bring to the publication.

Miranda McMinn on being a features editor

Miranda has worked as a features director for *Marie Claire* and *Red* and is a former associate editor of *Daily Express* Saturday magazine.

What are the everyday duties of a features editor?

Managing the features team, presenting the features list to the editor, chairing features ideas meetings, cultivating and commissioning writers and PRs, editing, tweaking headlines, working with the picture desk, and planning two or three issues ahead.

What ingredients make the perfect feature story?

Something that has a clear **angle** and preferably writes its own headline. It must have direct appeal that is specifically relevant to the title's readers, whether it's emotional, practical or spotting a trend.

What do you look for when reading a story proposal from a freelance?

A good story idea and a strong understanding of the title.

How do you prefer freelance writers to contact you and your publication?

By email. Contact the features secretary/editorial assistant to find out the best address to send ideas to. Be patient as all ideas need to be passed by the editor and it can take time for a features editor to get in to see them.

If you get the impression that your story isn't going to make it, then suggest that, while this is fine, you need to move it on elsewhere.

What was your first break in journalism?
I trained on the *Hendon & Finchley Times*, a local paper, then I moved onto newspapers and then into glossy magazines.

What advice would you give anyone hoping to get into magazines?
Do work experience for as long as you can. Shop around by doing a week here and there in a few places, then, when you find somewhere where you feel you fit in, understand the product and get on with the team, get your feet under the table and stay for as long as they will let you and as long as you can afford it.

I waitressed while I did work experience on local papers before finally being taken on as a trainee. There was a recession on and no jobs around, but I got there in the end although I shed a few tears of desperation along the way.

Commissioning editor

In a more junior editorial position than features editors, they are also involved in the commissioning and editing process. Commissioning editors are normally assigned sections or pages and may also be asked to edit other sections or contribute short articles.

Staff feature writer

Some writers are fortunate enough to be employed by their publication on a full-time basis, which means that they attend regular features meetings and contribute to appropriate parts of the publication. Staff writers are multi-taskers and should be able to write a snappy news story as well as an in-depth profile. They often cover specialist areas such as crime, foreign affairs or the environment.

Freelance writer

Although not normally on the payroll of any particular publication, a freelance can work for any number of editors. The most successful freelance writers contribute to dozens of publications on a regular basis.

They are paid a set word rate for their work, but this can be negotiated. Like staff writers, a specialist area of interest helps but good, reliable freelances can turn their hand to most subjects. Unlike staff writers, they rarely work in their publication's office, choosing instead to work from home or in a shared office with other freelances. See chapters 9 and 10 for more detailed information on freelancing.

Sub-editor

When it comes to proofing and editing incoming copy, the sub-editor (or 'sub') is the key member of the editorial team. Sub-editors report to the chief sub-editor on a large publication and also write headlines, **standfirsts** and picture captions.

Sarah Cooper on sub-editing

Sarah is a freelance sub-editor for various publishing companies, including *News International* and *Seven Squared*.

What are your normal hours?

I work eight hours a day, although it can be up to twelve hours if working for a newspaper and it's a print day.

What happens on a typical working day?

I usually get called in when print day is looming. This means my days are consistently busy and I rarely have the downtime that a staffer would experience.

My normal sub-editing duties include cutting copy to fit, writing headlines, standfirsts and captions as well as choosing appropriate **pull quotes** and fact checking. If I'm working for a company that I haven't freelanced for before, I familiarize myself with their style guide and correlate this with their publications.

What are the challenges and responsibilities of being a sub-editor?
You are responsible for bridging the gap between the editorial content and design. You must ensure the copy is as tight and accurate as it can be, and that it fits the design on the page.

What do you like most about sub-editing?
I like working with **InDesign** (page design software) and being involved with the production side of magazines. You can do some of this at home but it also allows me to work in an office, on defined shifts, and experience the buzz of a print day.

Are there any perks?
As a staffer, yes – first choice on the beauty cupboard's goodies!

ASK DAN

Do you need a degree or similar qualification to be a journalist?

Doing a journalism degree is undoubtedly a worthwhile preparation for a career in journalism and there are a number of recommended undergraduate courses on offer (see **Undergraduate courses**, p 140).

But while degrees are an advantage, they do not guarantee immediate or lasting success in the profession. Indeed, journalists come from all sorts of social and educational backgrounds and many of today's newspaper editors were cutting their teeth in the newsroom while their more educated contemporaries languished in university libraries and student union bars.

In theory, anyone with sufficient talent, drive or connections can succeed. You must show an above-average command of the English language and produce glowing copy that leaves readers and editors alike wanting more. If you do, it is unlikely that anyone will ask for evidence of your 'proper' education.

So media-friendly gardeners, globe-trotting foreign correspondents, sports pro-turned-pundits, celebrity gossip peddlers or ace music reviewers – you too have every chance of making it to the top.

Are journalists well paid?

There is indeed a select band of journalists who could describe themselves as being 'well paid' and you could include national newspaper and magazine editors, star columnists and high-profile writers among them. This fortunate minority command well over the magical 'pound per word', but the rest of us must settle for rather less.

Journalism will not make you stinking rich but it is a hugely rewarding and engaging career path to take which constantly sharpens the mind and changes your perspective on life. It also allows you to indulge in your favourite passions and interests. Always liked good wine? Establish yourself as a wine critic and have free bottles sent to your home address. Are you concerned about the environment? Then write about the issues that matter to you and see how your published work influences people all over the world.

Are there opportunities in journalism for people of different social and ethnic backgrounds?

Twenty to thirty years ago journalism was undoubtedly a club populated by white middle-class men – but then so was Britain.

Today, the picture could not be more different, with women either editing national newspapers or holding down senior editorial posts.

Black and Asian reporters are also becoming more visible in the mainstream media and there are dozens of ethnic and religious publications that reflect the increasing diversity of the UK's readership.

As our cultural diversity spreads further, editors will continue to look for reporters to reflect this in mainstream print and online media.

2

Who are you going to write for?

'Don't you see that today the boy wiped his feet on the choice, on the predilections of sixty million men and women of the greatest country in the world! If you had any morals yourself, you would understand the immorality of that boy's stand today! It was not me he criticized – it was my readers!'

Gossip columnist J.J. Hunsecker in Sweet Smell of Success

So you're a highly driven writer with bucketloads of story ideas and the ability to research, write and file pages of glowing copy. What can possibly stop you now?

All you have to do is persuade an editor to listen to your ideas and publish your work. No problem, you might think: there are hundreds of publications out there with pages waiting to be filled with your sharp observations and deft turns of phrase.

If only it were so simple.

Establishing yourself and surviving in journalism long term requires not only the creative element of finding good story subjects and writing them up, but also a highly detailed study of the markets you must deal with – in our case newspapers, magazines and online publications.

Clearly, it is impossible to keep regular tabs on *all* publications, either on the news stand or online, but having established the kind of things you are interested in writing about (music, health, personal finance, politics etc.) you can narrow down the markets or sectors that your writing should be directed towards.

Say, for example, you are keen on travel. Well, who isn't? You could start by looking at consumer travel magazines such as *Condé Nast Traveller*, *Sunday Times Travel*, *National Geographic* or *Wanderlust*. These, incidentally, are just a few of the many specialist travel magazines on show at the newsagent's.

Then there are the various magazines and national newspapers that publish travel writing (among other things) on a regular basis such as the *Guardian*, *Marie Claire*, *GQ* or the *Daily Mail*. Spread the net further and you have dozens of local papers with regular travel pages including the London *Evening Standard*, *Liverpool Echo* and the *Leicester Mercury*.

And if these aren't going to publish your stories, think about travel trade journals like *Travel Weekly* or *Travel Trade Gazette*. Failing that, try in-flight magazines like British Airways' *High Life* or *Voyager* by BMI. Or how about considering guide books, advertorial pages or brochures? All this, and we haven't even got as far as overseas publications or the internet!

The message which, hopefully, comes across here is that budding writers must spend a long time reading a variety of publications, many of which may not have previously entered their cultural orbit.

My first published story, complete with that all-important **byline** (or writer's credit), appeared in the hardly prestigious *Big Issue*, sold on the streets by homeless people. Incidentally, I was paid the grand total of £30. Yet as the story's subject matter concerned street graffiti, it seemed an appropriate enough publication.

Before this early professional triumph, I had hardly given the *Big Issue* a second look. Once I had familiarized myself with its content, however, I felt confident enough to follow my graffiti story up with a series of articles about notoriously rude (as in bad-mannered) establishments including a pub, a shop, a Chinese restaurant and a barber's. Although received enthusiastically enough by the *Big Issue*, my 600-word urban vignettes entitled 'Rude London' would not have been remotely

USA TODAY
NEWSLINE
ELECTION
THE Sun
MY STORY ...
EXCLUSIVE
HOL'S FOR £5
SUMMER
DER SPIEGEL
€
$
£
Le Monde

suitable for society bible *Tatler* or the stockbroker's favourite, the *Financial Times*.

Readers matter

Publishers and their editors are always trying to attract more readers, yet many struggle to determine who actually reads their publication and what they read in it.

A thorough knowledge of readers helps not only to focus the efforts of the publication's advertising department (the one which actually makes money for the publisher, remember) but to shape the editorial direction of the publication overall.

Say, for instance, you are editor of *Nursing Times*. It is practically a given that your readers work or are training to work in the nursing/healthcare sector. You can bet too that the majority of your readers are young professional women working for the NHS or in private medicine. A minority of them will be men.

Other than the responsibility of generating and overseeing regular content on the nursing profession, one of the good things about your job is that your readership is clearly defined and therefore you will be able to fill your pages with news stories and feature articles that directly address the concerns and interests of those readers.

This applies similarly if you are editing or writing for *Angling Times* (read by amateur fishing enthusiasts, mostly male and middle-aged), *The Lady* (nannies and carers, mostly female) or *Saga* (both male and female retirees from all over the UK).

Admittedly, the distinction is not quite so clear if you are editing *The Sunday Times* or *Daily Mail*, but you should at least have some information on the following points regarding your average reader:

1. The percentage of male and female readers
2. Their age range (e.g. 18–30 or 45–60)
3. Their social class
4. Their average income
5. Their level of education
6. The type of job they do
7. Where they live

You could of course take this a stage further and find out what they do at weekends, what car they drive or what TV programmes they watch (a recent *Daily Telegraph* reader survey even asked what cheese they favoured – 'Yes to Brie, no to cottage cheese' if you are interested).

The bottom line is that you, the editor or writer, have more than a basic understanding of what readers expect from your title and, furthermore, what they enjoy reading within its pages.

Remember that your publication should not only inform and entertain but should also be highly useful to specific groups of readers. And the more useful, urgent or essential the information is, the more likely it is that your readers will continue reading.

Getting to know them better

Newspaper and magazine advertising departments speak of ABC1s and C2Ds, which go some way to defining the social class, aspirations and spending power of your typical reader (see the chart on page 28).

Although undeniably a useful guideline, I have always preferred not to stereotype them like this. Full page advertisements and readers' letter pages, and sometimes even classified ads, offer an equally accurate insight into the cares and aspirations of your reader. Put crudely, a luxury watch ad in a glossy monthly denotes a high disposable income whilst a promotion for cut-price supermarket biscuits implies a budget-conscious housewife.

Whoever you end up writing for, try to visualize that person reading your article and put yourself into their shoes for a moment. Are they reading it on a crowded city train or over a relaxed weekend breakfast? Are they working or retired? Eco warrior or gas-guzzling road hog? Educated or uneducated? Politically left or leaning towards the right?

Even better, why not first write a short profile of your intended reader (just a few lines will do) and copy it to the top of your page just to remind you whose interests you are serving? Incidentally, as a journalist, you are definitely not serving your own; leave that to bloggers, Twitter-feed writers and novelists.

If, by this stage, you are still not clear who your reader is, then try the following:

1 Examine the media pack
Media packs are designed for the use of potential advertisers and contain useful facts and statistics about a publication's readers. Ask your target publication's advertising department to send you details or, if available, download one from their website.

Here's some useful information gathered from the media pack of women's weekly *Pick Me Up*:

Circulation: 374,288
Median age: 27
Children in household: 48%
Working: 50%
ABC1: 34%
Main shopper: 78%

(*Sources:* Target Group Index 2008; Audit Bureau of Circulation July–December 2008; National Readership Survey July–December 2008)

Assuming that you have never seen this magazine, let alone written for it, what can be deducted about our readers and their interests?

Perhaps the most significant point is that our typical reader is, more often than not, a young to middle-aged working mother from primarily a working-class background. Her main concerns are looking after her children and shopping for the family. From the magazine she expects real-life stories, bargain fashion ideas and puzzles. Editor June Smith-Sheppard calls it 'the real-life magazine with attitude and humour'.

Compare this profile to readers of *The Economist*, who according to its website are demographically broken down into ideas people, pioneers, catalysts and builders.

> 87 per cent of readers are male and their median age is 47 years.
>
> Their average household income is $243,000 and 52 per cent work for a market leading company. 85 per cent of readers took three or more return air trips last year.
>
> (www.theideaspeople.economist.com)

In case you haven't got the picture already, we are looking at an entirely different creature from our *Pick Me Up* buyer. In fact, looking at the data in more detail, it is hard to imagine these two specific groups of readers actually living on the same planet. Either way, it doesn't do any harm for writers to read their target publication and acquaint themselves with such details.

2 Go through recent issues

Examine advertisements, look at readers' letters or, if necessary, eavesdrop on readers' online chat rooms. Even a magazine's cover can say a tremendous amount about the reader's tastes, interests and aspirations. Note the age or attractiveness of the cover star, the boldness of the background colours or the style and cleverness of the cover lines.

3 Meet readers face-to-face

Most writers rarely meet their readers but they should, as it really would help them to direct their writing better. Other than catching them glancing at your article on a train (a rare occurrence in my experience), readers can be found at special reader events, promotions, focus groups and launch parties. And while they are there, ask them what they think of your publication and what pages they automatically turn to.

Which publications are you going to write for?

Now that you are better acquainted with your reader, it's time to decide which publications you are going to target. Most of us dream of writing for *The Sunday Times* or *Vanity Fair*, but in reality it's more likely to be *Grocer's Weekly* or *Insurance Broker's Monthly*.

Freelance writers normally try to attach themselves to three or four non-competing publications, and they should never turn down the opportunity to write for a new one. The most successful writers have their work published not only in national newspapers and monthly magazines but also overseas titles, websites, in-flight magazines, corporate brochures and travel guides.

Put simply, a prompt pay cheque always comes before the prestige and reputation of the publication in which the article appears.

Getting published and staying published is therefore not just a question of having a great writing ability and the sense of what makes a good story; it depends also on your capacity to research the market widely enough and being able to take advantage of new opportunities, such as the launch of a new title or a sudden change in the editor's chair.

This may all seem a bit daunting, but believe me it isn't. The best way to get the ball rolling is to focus on subject areas that interest you. Whether it's environmental issues, photography, health and fitness or model railways, you will find several publications dedicated to these interests. Start by picking up one or two titles from your nearest library or newsagent's (or otherwise browse their online versions) and begin to analyse them in a lot more detail than an ordinary reader would. Once you have done this, you will have a much clearer view of this sector overall, and one which will help you no end when it comes to pitching and writing stories to publications within it.

Once you've covered one sector (say, for instance, motoring publications), then move on to another subject area that interests you. There are all sorts of sectors out there to suit all popular tastes from computing, mountain biking or tattooing to social networking and knitting.

If there isn't a stand-alone publication, magazine supplement, website or newspaper section out there that reflects your specialist interest, then there soon will be. Publishers are a canny lot when it comes to making money.

For an extensive summary of the current UK and international newspaper and magazine market complete with up-to-date summaries and editorial contact details you could do worse than invest in a copy of the annual *Writers' & Artists' Yearbook*. I bought my first copy in 1994 and still find it an essential reference book when stuck for a publication in which to place a difficult story.

And as you begin to gather information on a wide range of publications, don't forget to update yourself on any important developments, whether it's a change in owner, editor or overall editorial policy. The publishing world is an increasingly dynamic one and today's publications are often unrecognizable from those that existed two or three years ago.

Remember, you should *never* approach a publication without having first familiarized yourself with its content.

National Readership Survey classification

This classification system was developed over fifty years ago and remains an effective way of classifying readers of different publications. Social grade is determined by the occupation of the chief income earner (CIE) in each household. Additional criteria, such as the size of the organization and the number of people for which the CIE is responsible, are used to refine the process.

Social grade	Social status	CIE's occupation
A	Upper middle class	Higher managerial, administrative or professional
B	Middle class	Intermediate managerial, administrative or professional
C1	Lower middle class	Supervisory or clerical and junior managerial, administrative or professional
C2	Skilled working class	Skilled manual workers
D	Working class	Semi and unskilled manual workers
E	Those at the lowest levels of subsistence	Casual or lowest grade workers, pensioners and others who depend on the state for their income

Exercise: Magazine analysis

Pick up a magazine you are interested in writing for and start this short exercise by filling in the details below. There are a few sub-headings to get you started. The same questions can be practically applied to any market sector, so don't stop at one or two publications:

Title (What's it called?)

Publisher (Who publishes it? See the **masthead** at the front)

Editor and features editor (These are the people who will commission your writing. They can also be found on the masthead)

Frequency (Weekly, monthly, quarterly?)

Formula/philosophy (What's its message or promise? For example, 'The sharper read for men')

Article types/average word length per article (What subjects are covered and in how much depth?)

Treatment and tone (Are the articles picture-led or wordy? Are they serious, fluffy or humorous in tone?)

Market competitors (You'll find these next to your publication on the news stand)

ASK DAN

How many publications is it possible to write for?

As a freelance there is no limit to the number of markets you can write for and a talented writer can soon develop a healthy portfolio of publications.

On the other hand, editors tend to disapprove of their writers contributing regularly to rival publications and they certainly don't want to be sold the same stories. For instance, you wouldn't approach rivals *GQ* and *Esquire* with the same men's interest piece. Likewise, it would be a bad idea to target the *Daily Mail* and *Daily Express* with similar feature stories.

Unfortunately, staff writers (staffers) do not have the same freedom as freelances, as they are contracted exclusively to their publication. In this instance, they must ask permission to be published elsewhere from their editor.

Do readers and their interests *always* dictate what I write about?

While the considerations of the average reader should be uppermost in any editor or writer's mind, content is also driven by the interests, knowledge, experience and aims of the individuals in the editorial team.

In other words, it is not always about what readers want to read, but what writers and editors *believe* they should be reading based on their knowledge and understanding of the publication.

As long as the subject matter and the way the story is presented fits the overall philosophy of the publication, your story is likely to appeal to those specific readers.

How do I know whether readers like my work?

Who says that readers have to *like* your work?

You can inform, amuse, infuriate or shock but as long as they are reading you and engaged by your writing you will continue to have a career in this profession.

Readers rarely comment directly to journalists but with more writers **blogging** or publishing their personal email address alongside their articles, this is becoming more commonplace. Journalism is an increasingly interactive profession, with plenty of opportunities for readers to comment.

Readers really do like to put writers in their place where necessary. In my career to date, I have been corrected several times, once by an ex-wing commander from Somerset who pointed out my incorrect use of the word 'pilot' – 'airman', he wrote, was the appropriate terminology.

3

What are you going to write about?

'What the man in the street wants to read is not what he has said already but what he would like to have said if he had thought of it first.'

Former Fleet Street columnist Keith Waterhouse

Once you have established what publications you want to write for, it's time to find some good, marketable stories that you can sell to them.

There is no magic formula, unfortunately, to unearthing the kind of story an editor might want to pick up and run with. Journalists get their ideas from all kinds of sources. But generally speaking, if you keep your eyes and ears open and follow up on *any* nugget of information that could possibly be of public interest, you are half way there.

As I said in Chapter 1, journalists by nature are inquisitive, interested in people and what affects them and, it has to be admitted, a little on the nosey side. If not, MPs would be still be getting away with outrageous expense claims and the plight of innocent terrorist suspects would go unnoticed by the world's media.

Practically anything you read in print or online has a convincing editorial reason behind it, whether it's the high-profile launch of a charity campaign, the results of a new health survey or the latest celebrity endorsement.

Below are ten tried and trusted methods of finding story subjects worth writing about. Remember also to keep an ideas notebook or palm-sized gadget handy for when inspiration strikes. After all, you don't want to see another hungry reporter get there first!

10 ways to find your story

1 Read a lot

Not just national and local newspapers but trade journals, ethnic and religious titles, free sheets, websites, blogs, letters pages etc.; any of the above will reveal information that might spark an idea for your feature story.

Articles that are best suited to following up with a more in-depth treatment include News In Brief stories (NIBs), gossip columns, business pages, regional and foreign news and even celebrity pronouncements on messaging service sites such as Twitter. Your article could even be triggered by a simple poster ad on a train platform or a flyer on a library notice board.

2 Listen

Whether it's a couple gossiping on the top deck of a bus, a comment at a dinner party or an interesting radio documentary, there are thousands of fascinating new subjects waiting to be written up for print and online publications.

All you need to do is keep your ears open and remember to follow up on any information that could lead to a potential news/feature story. Take note of any details and don't be afraid to ask other journalists for relevant contacts. What initially makes it into your ideas pad may never actually get off the ground, but if you spend time developing the essence of your idea, you will at least give it a chance.

3 Look ahead

Journalists need to know what is up-and-coming, not what has already passed. Read event listings publications such as *Time Out*, check ticket agency announcements or sign up to press alerts with arts and exhibition centres, record and film companies, book publishers, political parties, pressure groups etc. You should plan months ahead and remember that monthly magazines need to see your idea at least three months before going to press.

Obviously you are competing against experienced profile writers, news hacks and critics who will have this information to hand. It doesn't mean, however, that your story idea or approach must be the same.

4 Attend exhibitions, trade shows, lectures, conferences etc.

Even if you are not a fan of the arts or have never been to Olympia or the NEC, try to get into the habit of seeing what different organizations or manufacturers are planning. At a trade show everything is under one roof, so if you are an aspiring travel writer you can meet representatives of just about every tourist board in the world.

Likewise, if you regularly attend lectures at the Royal Geographical Society, you might just catch that exclusive talk by that internationally renowned zoologist.

Again, you can hear about such events by subscribing to in-house publications, checking up-to-date listings or contacting the organizer's press office directly. And while you are talking to them, don't forget to ask them to send you regular updates and press releases.

5 Indulge your interests

Aren't journalists supposed to write about what they know? Well, if your passion is gardening or you are obsessed with clothes, you can guarantee that these interests are widely represented in print and online media. Why not therefore play to your strengths and write for publications that cover these subjects?

Admittedly, journalism is not always the glamorous ride it appears to be, but at least its practitioners get to live out their fantasies on a regular basis. Just ask the football reporter who always gets World Cup final tickets or the arts reviewer who gets invited to the best private viewings at the Venice Biennale.

6 Write from experience

Use personal experiences or those of your family, friends and acquaintances. If it's happened to you, then it's probably happened to others who will share an affinity with your story subject. Were you bullied at school or married to an alcoholic? Then write these up as first person accounts or, otherwise, investigate these subjects in greater detail and see where it leads.

And, if your house gets repossessed and your valuables are removed by bailiffs, don't despair; this too is the platform for a potentially interesting piece of writing.

7 Follow up tip-offs, leads and rumours

Most stories you end up covering lead to information that could be used in a **follow-up** story. Whether you are interviewing a famous person or attending a book launch, someone in the room will be about to do something worth writing about. Only it's your job to write about it first.

8 Be open to new ideas, concepts and experiences

Just because you've never played a computer game before or grown your own vegetables on an allotment, it doesn't mean you can't write about it. As long as you can find people that *do* know what they are talking about (we call them 'experts'), you can at least develop a convincing story angle and begin your research.

Whether it's global financial markets or Japanese food, journalists tend to have a basic understanding of lots of different subjects, and this knowledge is picked up through an enquiring nature and a willingness to experience the world at large.

9 Target specific publications

You know what *you* want to write about, but what does your publication actually need? To find this out, read your target title in detail and find pages that rely on outside contributions. Perhaps there's a page on people with interesting professions (we all know someone with one of those!) or a slot in which celebrities talk about their favourite holiday. You could be just the person to conduct the interviews and write these stories up.

10 Develop useful contacts

Contacts can make or break a career and if you are in the habit of making new ones, you will find that stories will come to you. Whether your contact is a PR for a large company, a globetrotting freelance photographer, a young entrepreneur or a healthcare professional, all these different people can provide information that is potentially newsworthy.

Exercise: Finding feature stories from news items

See how many potential story ideas or angles you can find from the following short news items. To get you started, I have listed possible story suggestions for each:

1 Two Irish businessmen have been selling Irish soil to the American market. The dirt costs £8 for a 12oz bag. So far they have shipped over £530,000 worth of soil.
Possible story idea: a piece about how ex-pat communities identify with their homeland. To include case studies with Indians, Pakistanis, Australians and Poles living in the UK.

2 New research says that living in London 'speeds up the ageing process'. Pollution, smoking, stress and poor sun care are the contributing factors according to a study by a skin treatment firm.
Possible story idea: a debate piece for a women's monthly. A well-known city dweller argues the case for urban living against a famous champion for rural life.

3 Nearly a million British people gamble online says a government report. UK internet gambling has doubled in five years.
Possible story idea: an investigative feature on the effect of gambling on British households. Research will include interviews with addicts' families, colleagues and friends as well as comments from leading addiction experts.

How to place your story with the right publication

So you've made some useful contacts and have got into the habit of carrying an ideas book which is positively bulging with great news and feature stories. Now you just need to find a home for them.

Here's the bad news. Even experienced journalists have trouble interesting editors in publishing their work, so for the novice it's time to get real and accept that some of your stories just won't get off the ground.

Those with a clear target market have a head start, however, and a sharp awareness of different titles and their current content will ease the sometimes painful process of selling your story to an editor.

You should instinctively have a feel for which publication is the right one to approach. If you don't, this is a skill that, hopefully, you will develop over time.

Say, for instance, you want to write a piece about the pitfalls of adopting African orphans. It should be quite clear to you that the best market for this is a women's weekly, a Sunday newspaper supplement or possibly a parenting magazine. It should be obvious also that the subject matter is not remotely suitable for a teen or fashion title and you can discount these immediately.

Likewise, you can be sure that a story on eco-friendly bars belongs in the food and drink section of a Sunday newspaper and not a car or computing magazine.

The next trick is to know exactly where to pitch your story – if possible, right down to the precise section or page. By examining the market in closer detail you are not only widening the odds of your story being accepted, but finding new places where your writing might be published.

You should, by this stage, be clearer about what kind of article you are going to write. Is your story an in-depth profile, an opinion piece or a short news item? Your story subject and angle should guide you.

A proper journalist would never dare approach the editor of a title they had never even read, so familiarize yourself with any new title in detail, noting the page headings where your copy is most likely to appear. This doesn't count the gossip page ghost-written by the television soap star or the opinion column written by the media-friendly politician, but somewhere within its pages will be an opportunity for a hungry contributor such as yourself.

Knowing *when* to put your story forward to an editor is another consideration. You wouldn't suggest a piece on the attractions of Christmas street markets in the middle of summer (at least not to a daily newspaper). Likewise an investigative report into sleaze and corruption on the professional tennis circuit is probably best left until the build-up to Wimbledon – the exact time of year when practically everybody is focused on the game.

And if you can find a really convincing reason to run your story at a particular date (journalists call it a 'peg'), then you have doubled your chances of getting a commission.

Popular pegs include:

- linking to a current news story, report or survey
- the launch of something popular (film, book, television series etc.)
- linking to a major sporting, political or cultural event (the Olympic Games, G8 summit, Glastonbury festival etc.)
- major anniversaries (especially 1, 10, 50 or 100 years)
- linking to a celebrity (you'd be amazed how easy it is to do this)
- seasonal link (Christmas, school holidays, Ramadan etc.)

Exercise: Placing story ideas

Find specific publications and possible publication dates for the following stories:

1. An article on how to give up smoking
2. A story about the sharp increase in mature students at British universities
3. An investigation into solar powered transport
4. A first-person account of a British woman who left her family for a Turkish waiter while on holiday
5. A piece about how flirting with work colleagues helps you to climb the career ladder

Pitching your story

Whether you are a seasoned pro or a new kid on the block, there is no getting round the fact that you will have to pitch any new story idea to an editor.

A really hot news story such as the sighting of a high-ranking cabinet minister leaving a Soho massage parlour doesn't need much in the way of an explanation; a quick call to the all-too-eager news desk will do.

If, on the other hand, your story isn't the kind which demands the utmost urgency in terms of exposure or publication time, you may have to spell it out in more detail.

Timing is the key to most successful pitches, and if you can provide your editor with copy that he needs now (or at least *thinks* he needs now) you are on your way to your first commission.

In my earliest days as a freelance, I was left with no option but to cold call editors, and would be left practically speechless with nerves as they patiently ummed and ahhed as I struggled to interest them in my latest features proposal.

The alternative in those days was to send a brief fax message, but this didn't always arrive on the intended editor's desk and could at any time be picked up by a junior staffer and, God forbid, passed off in the next features meeting as their idea. Ideas, incidentally, cannot be copyrighted, so you are taking a chance by giving out information to anyone other than the intended editor.

Nowadays, of course, we don't actually need to *speak* to any editor if we don't want to. We send our story outlines via email and await their reply in the hope of a commission. I have been selling stories consistently to some editors that I have never even met, let alone spoken to, yet the professional relationship hasn't necessarily suffered.

What they are interested in is your story, not you, so try to spell it out as clearly and quickly as you can. Remember, editors are stressed-out and busy people and in the context of them editing new copy, commissioning high-profile writers, attending meetings and dealing with floods of PR calls, your story proposal is pretty low down on the list.

By all means call an editor if you truly have the confidence in your story and your ability to sell it. In reality, however, this is an undeniably daunting prospect for unpublished writers. Editors too tend to be reluctant to hear from as yet unknown or aspiring freelances.

In this case it is advisable to send them a short email message outlining your idea and approach. Three or four paragraphs should do it. Any more, and your already overburdened editor will switch off and delete.

Writing attention-grabbing story outlines

A successful story pitch will immediately attract an editor and outline the essence of your story clearly. You don't need to go into great detail but you should include the most important points.

Show them that you have sufficient knowledge of this subject and that you are absolutely clear about how it will be written.

Your language in the pitch should be upbeat and economical, certainly not long-winded and over-padded, demonstrating also that you are serving the reader's interests or tastes.

Here's a successful pitch to the health and fitness supplement of a leading daily broadsheet newspaper.

> Dear (add editor's name)
>
> I wondered if you'd like a piece on British Military Fitness (BMF), the latest fitness craze to hit parks up and down the country this summer.
>
> Set up by Major Robin Cope, BMF is the perfect antidote to the boring and expensive gym. The emphasis is on team spirit, drills, running and, naturally, press-ups. The trainers come from the armed forces including the Royal Marines, and some are from the elite Army Physical Training Corps.
>
> Despite its boot camp credentials, BMF is open to anyone (male and female, young or old) and classes take place in healthy open air spaces such as city parks. They are currently operating in London, Glasgow, Edinburgh, Manchester, Brighton, Cardiff and Guildford.
>
> I join a class to find out the appeal of BMF and see how it compares to my local gym. The article will include some background on the organization and an interview with its founder Major Cope.

Analysis

The writer certainly doesn't waste words getting to the heart of the story's subject and they provide sufficient background information for an editor to understand the concept.

Note the urgency of this story – it's a summer fitness craze and therefore the story must run in the near future otherwise its novelty value will be redundant. The editor also now knows that these classes take place all over the country, which means that readers can do this themselves. This is vital information for a story such as this.

The final paragraph outlines the writer's intention to try it personally, thereby adding an appealing first person element to the story. The proposed interview with Major Cope is a bonus and should impress the editor further.

Note: when promising interviews such as this, be clear whether you can deliver them or not. Individuals and organizations will often want to know whether you have been formally commissioned to write the story before giving up their valuable time.

If you haven't interested an editor at this stage, be clear to them who the story is intended for (*Daily Telegraph* Weekend section, *Time Out*, *Marie Claire* etc.) as opposed to 'I might get in published in …' or 'I'm sending it to …'

As soon as an editor becomes interested in your idea, you can begin to drop the name of their publication, which normally acts as a strong incentive to interviewees, especially those who seek publicity on a large scale. On the whole, a chance for them to speak to a national newspaper is far more enticing than appearing in a low-circulation specialist title or unheard-of website.

The above example also shows that the story's subject is ideal for an upmarket weekend health and fitness supplement and there is an excellent chance that readers will be interested in this trend.

Your pitch needn't be for a one-off story like the above. Provided your creative juices are flowing sufficiently, it is a good idea to target specific editors with several ideas at once. This can be an effective way of getting at least one commission, as your editor is able to pick and choose from a list. Unlike the above example, these outlines can be even briefer. Give each one a catchy title if possible (nothing too obscure) and put forward the main points clearly.

Here's an example of three separate stories pitched to the London *Evening Standard*'s travel pages:

Hostels de Luxe

Youth hostels aren't the cold and comfort-free walker's refuges they once were. The UK Youth Hostel Association (YHA) now offer a wide range of accommodation including mansions, lodges, cottages, and even tipis for those who want to sleep under the stars.

Locations are more varied than before and three-star urban YHAs are also planned. Many of their guest houses are designed for group hire and are equipped with all mod cons. One even comes with its own swimming pool.

Holiday Home Swap

Would you trade your Victorian semi for a Californian beach hut? Your chic urban loft for a classic French farmhouse?

My story is about the rise of international home exchange. Once the preserve of cash-strapped academics, now everybody seems to be enjoying the benefits of exchanging their home with a foreign family.

It is a fun and affordable alternative to booking a hotel or villa, and for longer stays there are numerous advantages such as car sharing, friendly neighbours, comfort, sharing cultures etc.

This is essentially a 'how to' piece, looking at which companies offer this service and what kind of properties you can expect to find. To find out what it's like, I'll be speaking to families such as the Ronsons from Kingston who swap homes regularly.

Open Water Swim

For those whose idea of a holiday dip means crossing choppy Mediterranean straits or, in the style of Lord Byron, swimming from island to island, UK-based Swim Trek (the world's only swimming adventure company) offers guided swimming/walking tours in a variety of stunning locations.

This year they are going to Greece, Croatia and Turkey, as well as home destinations such as the Isles of Scilly, the Lake District and the Thames.

I join a trip to Malta and go bay hopping and cliff swimming, ending up in Comino's famous blue lagoon.

Alternatively you could suggest a series of articles written by you on a specific subject. Editors are always looking at new ways to fill their pages, not just for their next issue but for the weeks, months or possibly years ahead. If you are the sort of person that can make their job easier, then you are more likely to have a successful long-term relationship.

Here's an example. Having had my first article on graffiti published in the *Big Issue*, I immediately followed this up with a call to the section editor about a possible series on the rudest-mannered establishments in town. I already had a piece written about a truculent pair of south London barbers but also knew of a notoriously abrupt landlord and a terrifying Chinese restaurant.

The column entitled 'Rude London' ran regularly for several weeks before I ran out of unpleasant shopkeepers and publicans, but the point is that I was able to turn a one-off story into a series of articles.

Every subject worth writing about must be treated in a similar way, and if you are looking to survive in journalism, this kind of approach is essential.

10 ways to write a successful story outline

1. Tell the essence of the story idea clearly
2. Be brief and to the point
3. Show enthusiasm and expertise (this comes through your initial research)
4. Provide enough background information (but not too much)
5. Show a clear story angle (how you are going to approach your subject)
6. Make it clear why this subject is relevant now
7. Use celebrity names or link to a recent report or survey if relevant
8. Give precise details (names, dates, times). Never be vague
9. Indicate *how* you intend to write it (interview, fly on-the-wall observation etc.)
10. Indicate a possible publication date and when you intend to deliver your copy

ASK DAN

Do I really need to send in a story pitch? Can't I just send in my finished manuscript?

Sorry, but unsolicited manuscripts rarely get published. This is because editors usually know what they are looking for and plan ahead accordingly.

If you are convinced enough of your writing ability to send copy in **on spec**, at least show that you are familiar with the publication's style and write strictly to the word length of the articles within.

When is the best time to pitch to an editor?

Editors are always on the lookout for new ideas, especially when their regular features meetings are about to begin.

But before picking up the phone or firing off that email message, bear in mind that they'll want to be contacted during one of their quieter, more contemplative moments. For a newspaper editor, that means well after the daily copy **deadline** has passed (usually after 4 p.m.).

Magazine editors have rather less pressing deadlines but are in meetings a lot. Generally speaking, before 11 a.m. and after 4 p.m. are the best times to bend their ear.

How do I know who is the most appropriate person to pitch my story to?

You can't just send your idea to 'the editor'. Unless it is a small publication, editors are often far too senior to deal with ambitious new freelances. Instead, examine the publication thoroughly and find out who edits the section you are targeting. Their name should be listed towards the head of the section or in the editorial team's **masthead** near the front.

Alternatively, telephone the publication directly and ask the switchboard operator or junior editorial assistant to tell you. Make sure you copy their name down correctly. Getting an editor's name wrong will hardly endear you to them.

If my piece is accepted, what kind of things must I check with my editor?

Your priority is to check how many words are required, what your story angle is and when you need to file it. Questions about money can come later. You can negotiate a fee and any expenses to be incurred if relevant, but don't let financial issues get in the way of your working relationship at this stage.

Do bear in mind that editors often expect you to change your story angle for them. If you want to work for them again, deliver what *they* want, not what you think will work best.

Say, for instance, you are interviewing a rock band, and they only want a short interview with the singer focused on his favourite gastronomic experiences, then do it. Your potentially more interesting piece with a music theme can be offloaded to another publication.

4

Writing it up

'Journalism is 50 per cent travelling, 40 per cent hanging around and 10 per cent frenetic activity. And in the hunt for information and the scramble for technical facilities, the story is often scribbled in minutes.'

BBC foreign correspondent Orla Guerin

Having found a suitable place for your story, now it's time to get down to the real business of researching and writing it.

With a promising story angle and the approval of an editor, not to mention the prospect of a byline and that first pay cheque, it's tempting to get all those words down as soon as you can. But wait.

At this stage it's probably a good idea to reassess these two questions:

1 What kind of story are you writing?
2 How much research do you actually have to do?

Article types

Whether it appears on a live news website or in the pages of a long-established monthly publication, there's a fair chance that your story will slot into an already existing or standard story type.

Say, for instance, you are going to write up that story on solar powered transport from the exercise in the last chapter. Do you see this as a long investigative piece or a straightforward motoring review? Perhaps it is best treated as an opinion piece or maybe there's a profile possibility here with the vehicle's designer.

As discussed previously, there are many ways to treat your story, so before beginning your research in earnest, make sure you are aware of the creative ambition and limits to this piece of writing.

Knowing this will not only help you to focus on the appropriate aspects of your story subject, but it might also save you from doing an unnecessary amount of fact gathering, interviewing or digging for background information.

The most typical published article types are:

News article: focuses purely on the latest facts with minimal description or colour.
Feature article: more developed, in-depth and analytical than a straight news story, often with a strong human interest.
Profile: the focus is on a newsworthy individual revealing their professional and personal background.
Review: shows the release or availability of an artistic or commercial endeavour and helps readers decide on its quality.
Opinion piece: a writer airs his or her views on a current topic.
Editorial: the official viewpoint of the publication on a current topic.

As a rule, feature articles take longer to research than short news items or opinion pieces. For a start, your word count will tend to be higher, often up to 2000 words in length. To write a piece like this properly you will need to interview several key people in order to find enlightening and up-to-date information on a subject that you may have little or no knowledge of.

On top of this you will be dealing with organizations and their PRs (some of whom may not want the coverage anyway) and you may also have to attend a conference, a demonstration or other event that is relevant to the story. Remember, all of these can take up a lot of your professional or personal time and, if taken to its extreme, may prevent you from moving onto other story opportunities.

An opinion piece, on the other hand, may demand no more research than a cursory glance at a selection of the day's newspapers. Once you have decided what you want to say and how you are going to say it, all you need is relevant facts or **quotes** to illustrate your points.

Before really rolling up those sleeves, therefore, it's worth considering how much research you actually need to do. Consider your story's subject, article type, anticipated word count, depth or treatment.

How to research your article

Strong, memorable news and feature stories – the kind that topple corrupt governments or alert us to some previously unheralded human plight – are invariably backed by proper research. Not the exhaustive, meticulous kind that a scientist or academic would conduct, but enough for the journalist to understand the subject sufficiently and convince the reader of their angle or viewpoint. Accuracy and supplying the very latest facts or statistics don't do any harm either.

No story I have ever written requires an exact amount of research. Sometimes you spend weeks cultivating contacts, poring over reports, or even infiltrating organizations to get your story, while at other times you get by on information found quickly and conveniently on the phone or via the internet.

Let's consider some popular research methods and assess their usage.

The internet

The net arguably a great starting point for any type of research, whether it's reading up on a celebrity you are about to interview or swotting up on the latest health scare for a news report. Many journalists use online encyclopaedias to get a basic handle on their subject or use search engines to track down experts or case studies. Short interviews are increasingly done via an exchange of email messages.

All this improves the overall speed of research, which is undoubtedly a good thing for both journalists and the publishing industry.

Beware: an over-dependence on search engines, websites and online encyclopaedias also has its drawbacks, notably the proliferation of second-hand and often second-rate information.

First-hand interviews

These form the foundations of your story. Imagine you are writing up the story on British Military Fitness (from Chapter 3). You will almost certainly be speaking to the founder, Major Cope, asking him about how and why he set up the organization. You might also want to go along to a session and while you are there chat to the instructor who will give you more insights into the organization. Before you go, why not talk to some other punters and find out what they thought of it?

If you are interviewing a famous actor, an informal chat with a co-star or old school friend also counts as research, and not all of it needs to be quoted verbatim.

Observation

Whether you are an undercover participant or fly-on-the-wall observer, there is no denying the effectiveness of experiencing something for yourself and noting your surroundings in detail. That means lots of army push-ups if you are covering the British Military Fitness story! This could also mean following a politician on a campaign trail or visiting the scene of an earthquake. In all these cases you are gathering unique and vital first-hand information for your story.

Contacting organizations

You cannot be expected to do all the work on your own and, nine times out of ten, you will be helped on your way by the press officers of the organizations you are writing about.

If researching the British Military Fitness story, it is likely that their press office or PR will set up everything up for you, including interviews and a session with an instructor.

In other instances the relevant press office might provide recent reports or surveys for you to look at. They might also provide other useful contacts that could be relevant to the story. In our army fitness story this might include a physical fitness specialist, doctor or serving army professional.

Background reading

You've done some initial reading up on your subject via the internet or press releases but why not broaden your research further?

Reading relevant newspaper and magazine articles all counts as research (if you miss them, they can often be found on their sister websites), as do factual books such as biographies or travel guides.

Indeed, the wider your reading is, the more likely that you'll find something more unusual, and thereby more entertaining, to work into your piece. There's no reason at all why you cannot quote a famous philosopher in a football report. This will separate you from the rest of the pack.

Standard research books for journalists include the local telephone directory, an atlas, anniversaries book and media guides. These should never be far from your desk.

Knowing where to find the information quickly is the key to effective research; once a good contact is made, be sure to keep it for future reference. Useful organizations for researching your article might (depending on your subject area) include the Department for Business, Innovation and Skills, the Arts Council, the House of Commons and the Office for National Statistics.

To conclude, here's a point about over-researching – too much detail might cloud an otherwise interesting read. It is your job to get up to speed on your subject then write the story in an authoritative way. Do not feel that you have to cram everything in to impress a reader. Indeed, knowing what to leave out is often the key to good feature writing.

Exercise: Research methods

Think about how you would start researching the following articles. In each case, try to list specific organizations, known contacts, websites or reference books.

1 An investigation into illegal drug use in the fashion industry
2 A story about the revival of urban allotments
3 An anniversary piece on the Girl Guide movement

Feature writing – the essentials

What makes an interesting read? Is it the story's subject matter, the use of language and dialogue, the colourful characters, observant descriptions or a combination of all these?

Every reader will have a different opinion on this, but now you are in a position to write up your story, let's examine how the professionals go about this form of writing.

As in any literary form (novel, film script, play, formal letter etc.), feature writing has its own set of rules, and if you are thinking about submitting articles to print and online publications you will need to accept them.

Personally, I think that feature writers need to entertain and amuse as well as inform and educate. Today we are faced with such a torrent of news print and online content that it is easy for readers to be turned off by seemingly endless amounts of text. The challenge for writers therefore is to break through this complacency and get readers to actually read, in full, what you have written.

How often have you yourself flicked through a publication only to glance at the pictures and captions or skim through an item that caught your interest only to drop it after a few paragraphs?

In your own publication, too, there is much to distract the attention away from your words. Pictures and captions aside, there are the TV listings, weather forecasts, puzzles, not to mention ads, readers' letters or blogs. Who said a writer's life was easy?

Story structure

Before putting all those words together, think hard about how your story will pan out. All articles start with an intro then flow into the main body **copy** before reaching a conclusion (a sequential beginning, middle and end, if you like).

Go through your notes again and pick out the bits (including facts, statistics and quotes) that best support your story angle. Don't be tempted to deviate from this.

Before you start writing, you should list the key points, preferably at the top of the page, to remind you what elements of the story you are dealing with and in what precise order. Say, for instance, it's a story on hot air ballooning, you might have the following guide points:

Intro
Who does it
What they say about it
Background to ballooning
Where to do it
How to do it – tips from an expert
Ending.

Now you can begin to write your copy under these subheadings, editing along the way and making sure the last line of every paragraph links effectively to the start of the next. Remember that each paragraph (ideally 2–3 sentences in length) should deal with a different point. Extra special attention is needed for your **intro** and ending, but more on that later.

Use of language

The way you write it should be clear and easily accessible to your reader. I know it's tempting, but try to avoid the kind of long, multi-syllable words that you might find in literary criticism or academic texts. Short familiar ones will do.

Other no-nos include clichés (crystal clear, hot favourite, shining example etc.), over-cooked or rambling sentences, unexplained jargon and the excessive use of adjectives. Don't even think about using an exclamation mark unless it's part of a quote.

Your job is to ensure that the reader's eye glides effortlessly from the opening paragraph to the final conclusion. If anything is unclear or unexplained, you will lose them straight way.

Note: over fifty years ago, the journalist and writer George Orwell said that 'the slovenliness of our language makes it easier for us to have foolish thoughts' (*Politics and the English Language*). He's still right, of course.

Style

In what style will you be writing it? You may be half way to developing your own writing style but be guided first by the **house style** of the publication you are writing for. Many publications have basic guidelines on how to approach numbers, dates and punctuation marks, but may also touch on ministerial titles or use of Americanisms. *The Economist* has its own style book, for instance, designed to guide potential contributors on topics ranging from international currency to yachting abbreviations.

The best way, of course, to understand your publication's style is to read it regularly. Styles can range from the **tabloid**-esque and gossipy to the technical or highbrow, and most people should be able to distinguish between the diverse editorial styles of *Tatler*, *Wired* and the *Daily Star*.

Accuracy

You are a journalist and so you are being paid for getting your facts right. When writing any piece of journalism there is no excuse for misspelt names and places or wrong dates, times and telephone numbers.

Don't leave it to someone else (such as the sub-editor) to clean up your mistakes. Practically everything in your story can be checked, either by a quick call to your original source or by going online.

Catchy intros

It's worth spending a bit of time on these, and the right intro will set up your piece nicely and act as an accessible way in for readers.

If well done, it will grip them sufficiently to carry on reading. Make sure it sparkles sufficiently and grabs their attention. There are no hard and fast rules for intro writing but you might want to consider the following:

Using eye-catching facts and figures: A million jobs will be created in the leisure industry next year. (article on future jobs)
Asking a provocative question: Where would we be without the black cab? (article on London taxis)
Using a striking or controversial quote: 'One guy had a heart attack right in front of me – the b****** never even paid me for the haircut.' (article on £1 barber shops)
First-person narrative: I first clapped eyes on my new flatmates as I stumbled in one rainy night last September … (article on the rise in domestic mice infestations)
Description: It came towards me, propelled by tracks on its feet, its emotionless face emitting a deafening siren … (article on vintage toy robots)

Your intro may not come to you immediately, so if you are stuck, read through an initial draft copy and see if any of your paragraphs might work further up the text. You can drop readers straight into the action or lead them in gently, make them feel uncomfortable or make them laugh. The subject matter and article length will dictate your approach.

Effective endings

If you're going to spend time working on your intro, don't forget to round it up neatly with a suitably clever ending.

It's no good just trailing off when you feel like it. Endings should leave the reader feeling entirely satisfied that your article has come to its conclusion.

A summary of your findings or a pithy comment usually suffices, but you can also end with a quote or a question, or otherwise refer directly back to your intro for inspiration. If your piece has a slightly campaigning tone (perhaps it's on the importance of women having a screening for breast cancer) then you might want to provoke the reader directly into action.

People

All news is essentially about people (as opposed to organizations, inanimate objects and abstract concepts). So when writing on any issue, the journalist must find the relevant personalities and include their actions and opinions in their story.

It's no good just listing facts – leave that to report and survey compilers. Your story will reach another level by the gathering of first-hand observations and quotes. These might be from the story's protagonists but also relevant commentators or experts in the field.

Take the quotes out of the average 1000-word feature for instance and it will be a rather flat, disappointing read. Quotes, especially hard-hitting, controversial ones, will really lift your story and help personalize it. Warning: do not get into the habit of over-relying on quotes or failing to edit them properly.

Exercise: Getting the right quotes

Who would be the best people to quote in the following stories? Give full names if possible. Explain your reasons and how you would use this person in your story.

- You are writing about a local church whose trendy young vicar has allowed aspiring young DJs to use the church hall
- You are writing a piece on a proposed parking toll for London cyclists
- You are writing a 'how to' piece about keeping a parrot. Is it even possible to find a celebrity quote here?

Edit it down

Even experienced writers end up writing several drafts before filing their piece. Initially, it is a case of reading your draft through and deciding how it can be made clearer and more understandable.

You'll need to check also that your story is properly constructed and logical in its development.

That means tidying up loose sentences, checking grammar, tenses and spelling as well as eliminating any unnecessary words and ridding it of clichés and technical/professional jargon. At this point, you should be asking yourself 'Is this entertaining/interesting/shocking/revealing enough?' and 'How can I improve this even more?'

Other considerations include tweaking it to fit into your publication's style. Does it have the right tone and does it use the right points of reference? Name dropping British soap stars is no use in an article for the *New Yorker*; likewise the intricacies of Wagner's Ring Cycle have no place in the entertainment pages of *Heat* magazine.

Above all, you should be thinking like an editor with an editor's detachment from the actual writing process. Ask yourself in all honesty 'Is this good enough as it stands?' then make the necessary changes without spoiling its original feel.

Filing copy

Always check with your commissioning editor what format your copy is required in.

The copy should be presented on a separate Word document (not pasted onto an email page) then sent as an email attachment.

The editor and sub-editor will then read it on the screen, or, if it's a longer piece, print it up as hard copy.

Any page of hard copy should carry your full name, publication and date of issue at the top left hand side. This makes it simple for the sub-editor to identify. A **catchline** or short word to identify the story should go at the top right hand corner, e.g. 'blast' in the case of a story about a household gas explosion.

You should leave a space between every line and two spaces between paragraphs so the sub can write their marks and comments alongside. To indicate that the story continues onto another page put 'mf' (more follows) at the bottom right of the page. The final page should carry the word 'Ends' to show that the piece is complete. A final word count, usually at the bottom left of the page, also makes a sub's job easier.

Try to avoid fancy fonts (Arial or Times New Roman will do) and don't forget to keep a copy for yourself as editors and sub-editors are notorious for losing copy in the system. As a writer of copy, you do *not* get involved with headline writing or supplying photographs and captions; leave it to the publication's sub-editor or photographer.

Be prepared, even at this late stage, to make changes. Stories, especially in news, often move on quickly and need updating. Above all, make sure you are satisfied you have done your job professionally. Your next commission may depend on it.

10 points to consider before filing your copy

1. Always address the concerns, interests and tastes of your reader
2. Write in a concise, economical style
3. Provide enough background information for your reader
4. Be enthusiastic and positive about your subject
5. Show readers that you know what you talking about
6. Include facts and statistics that are new, interesting or unusual
7. Make your story as topical and as newsworthy as possible
8. Let experts and commentators explain any complexities or jargon
9. Ensure that your story makes a specific point and stick to it
10. Choose strong verbs over neutral ones (e.g. *grip* as opposed to *hold*).

ASK DAN

What is meant by a 'good story angle'?

Your angle is the way you choose to treat the subject. Whether it's violence in schools, religious fundamentalism, eco transport or CCTV cameras, you need to say something new and specific about it.

Say, for instance, you want to write about violence in schools. You do a bit of research on the subject, then find out that there is a new government initiative aimed at teaching teenagers self-defence – that's your angle, and you must uncover this story in detail.

Likewise, eco transport is far too generalized a concept to take on in a newspaper or magazine article. Yet if you learn that a new solar powered passenger plane is in commercial development, then you may be able to write a piece espousing its potential virtues for air travellers.

How many edits do you normally need to do?

Two to three drafts is usually enough. The first is for simply getting the body copy down on paper and reaching the approximate required word rate.

Having read this through, you might want to make structural changes or rewrite the odd paragraph or two, especially the intro or ending.

This is a good moment also for checking that everything flows properly. Each paragraph must effortlessly link to the next.

Finally, you'll need to check details such as names, places, web addresses etc. This can be more time-consuming than it looks. Unless your editor has said otherwise, make sure that the final word count matches your agreed word count at the commissioning stage. If they want 600 words, don't send 656 and expect them to trim it down for you.

How do I find my own distinct writing voice?

A distinct writing voice is what every journalist secretly yearns for. Few are born with one, but if you are true to yourself and continue to respect the basic rules of journalism, you will inevitably find one.

When starting out, it's not a bad thing to emulate the style of your heroes – John Pilger, Julie Burchill, and Jeremy Clarkson are all perfectly acceptable role models, but essentially it's your own personality and interests that you want to shine through.

Best-selling author Andy McNab says that a good technique is to write as if you are telling a story to your mate in a pub. The point here is that you should be relaxed and true to yourself, not pretentious and long-winded. And if you are pretentious and long-winded, good luck in getting your stories published!

My basic English is not good enough. How can I improve my grammar, spelling and punctuation?

Just because your English isn't perfect, it doesn't mean that you won't make a good journalist. Integrity, drive and good people skills may also help you along the way. You'll be surprised also how many top writers and editors fail to grasp the basics in English grammar and syntax.

That said, there is no getting round the fact that journalism is one profession that requires an above-average command of the language, and if your spelling is not up to scratch or you have trouble with capital letters and punctuation you will get found out.

Brush up on your grammar skills with a textbook such as the *Longman Guide to English Usage* or go to an online learning site such as www.bbc.co.uk/skillswise. Otherwise enrol in an evening class. Reading a lot, especially the quality newspapers, is another enjoyable way of improving your English.

5

Profiles and celebrity stories

Interviewing is about listening rather than asking questions. Of course you do have to ask questions, but only the bare minimum to get them going.

Observer *and* Sunday Times *profile writer Lynn Barber*

Profile writing is regarded as a highly specialized area of journalism and there are few writers who do this really well. Despite this, most journalists are expected to conduct an in-depth interview or two at some stage of their career.

When we think of published interviews, glossy magazines usually spring to mind. The majority of monthly magazines and Sunday supplements swear by the celebrity profile and the right face on the cover can boost **circulation** figures and enhance a publication's reputation within the industry. When an interview goes down well, it is not only the celebrity that benefits; the writer's credibility also rises.

Similarly, magazine editors spend months planning cover shoots with the hottest new stars, knowing that an exclusive interview will mean far more than a pat on the back from their publisher.

But it's not just classic celebrity cover stories that keep profile writers busy. Profiles and personality-led interviews crop up in all sorts of publications and their inner sections.

Your next profile piece, for instance, could be with a new mover and shaker in the business world or with a much-talked-about gardener. It could be an ordinary person who has witnessed something extraordinary (such as a terrorist attack or plane crash) or perhaps a member of the public who has recently been in the news or has something interesting (or possibly scandalous) to say about a somewhat better known person.

The platform for profile writing is increasingly varied too. The standard celebrity profile records the meeting of the personality and the writer, often setting the scene before the dialogue begins. Others rely purely on the questions (the Q&A approach), which can be effective if the celebrity has rejected the suggestion of a face-to-face meeting, or the interview has a special focus such as taste in food, media or holidays.

Otherwise your profile could take the first-person approach in which your interview subject tells *their* story with your expert assistance. These kinds of stories are popular in women's weekly magazines ('I married a monster', 'I lost 50 kilos in six months' etc.) and are read by millions.

On a practical level, writing a profile piece can involve anything from jetting out to Los Angeles to meet an A-Lister face to face or, at the other end of the spectrum, emailing a list of questions to the agent of a rising comedy star in the hope that they will say something amusing in your regular column.

Before setting yourself up as a profile writer, you must ask yourself whether you really have an innate interest in people and what makes them tick. If you don't, you might find profile writing a bit of a bore. Once you have got over the initial thrill of being in a room with a famous person, trust me, it isn't as exciting as it's made out to be.

You must also share the natural curiosity of your **readership** and desire to know 'what goes on behind the curtains?'

Successful profile writers also have a knack of finding good interview subjects. These can come from any walk of life, not just from the telly or big screen, but their underlining appeal will be their relevance to the publication you are writing for. Upmarket men's magazines, for example, invariably like to interview rising film starlets (preferably French) or the latest incarnation of James Bond. More downmarket men's titles, meanwhile, go for semi-clad Big Brother contestants or models otherwise seen in the pages of tabloid newspapers.

If your heart is set on interviewing rock stars, then you will need to start cultivating contacts with their agents, managers and gig promoters fast. This applies to practically any area of interest, the trick being at this stage to identify people who are 'on the up' in their profession.

Those who have already got there are often far too important to talk you, or indeed to any established profile writer. Whether they are footballers or film stars, household names are increasingly reluctant to yield to the traditional interview experience; they don't have to, as they increasingly have their own media outlets to do this.

This leaves the would-be profile writer having to search further afield, which is no bad thing actually. Better to find an enthusiastic and open-minded star of tomorrow than go through the exhausting, time-consuming process with a jaded has-been.

Setting up the interview

By and large, profiles are published for a particular reason, not simply because editors feel like having them in their publication.

The reason, or **peg**, for a profile **piece** is usually the launch of a new film, a high-profile product endorsement, a charity launch or publication of a book. It is the personality's agent who contacts the journalist (or the other way round) about the possibility of an interview with their client. This must be arranged weeks or months before launch date to allow for the publication's lead time. In the case of consumer magazines, this can be up to three months ahead.

Otherwise journalists must dig around for suitable interview subjects themselves. These are found by regularly reading the newspapers (the entertainment and gossip pages are especially good for hearing about the latest films or television productions) or listings guides.

Magazines cultivate particularly close relationships with celebrity agents and subscribe to celebrity-led listings services for information on forthcoming film/book/television/music releases.

Alternatively, look to your own hard-won contacts. Say, for instance, you are a new technology writer, financial journalist or a health and fitness correspondent. Surely you have come across someone interesting and media-friendly who would make for an interesting in-depth profile?

If you are hell-bent on celebrity interviews then charities and commercial sponsors are an increasingly effective route to the stars. The star may not be keen to speak to a low circulation title such as yours about their new film, but only too happy to speak up on behalf of Friends of the Earth or Cancer Research. Make sure you credit the organization and its work in the finished piece.

The interview process

Where to meet

If the agent or PR company controls the logistics of the interview, it invariably means you are allotted a limited time with their client, usually in a

hotel lobby or room in their offices. Incredibly, many high-profile interviews are squeezed in via 10-minute phone calls or during chauffeured journeys on the way to and from airports.

These are not the most ideal circumstances for the journalist or the reader; other profile writers will invariably be getting the same treatment and the end results tend to be bland and samey.

If, however, you can get your subject away from their normal celebrity environment, you have a better chance of extracting something different. Getting George Clooney to have a drink with you in your local pub is asking a little too much perhaps, but you never know – he might be glad of a change of scene.

For all face-to-face interviews, avoid rowdy bars or restaurants where members of the public will keep coming over and interrupting. Unless your interview slot is called 'A Night on the Town with …' then ask your questions during normal office hours. Too early in the morning is also a bad idea, as both interviewer and interviewee may not be at their most loquacious.

Be prepared

Having arranged the date, time and place with your interview subject, it's time to speed up your research on them. If they are well known, read up about them in a variety of publications – that means tabloids and weekly magazines as well as serious papers and news weeklies.

The point here is that you are working towards establishing your own original angle. What do you want to say about this person and how are you going to support your comments? The best interview articles have a clear and consistent theme, e.g. Is X a better singer without drugs? or Is Y happier now she has a young family?

Detailed questions are not necessary at this stage, but you should be thinking of the kind of things you want to ask. This also eliminates the need to answer questions that you know already. There is nothing more deflating for a celebrity than to be asked the same question over and over again or to explain something that has already been explained dozens of times before.

Other valid research before the interview takes place includes reading their official biog (their agent will be happy to oblige) or chatting to their professional or personal friends and acquaintances. The more angles you can get on your subject the better, and hopefully you will be striving to avoid the bland biographical guff that you normally find on an official or fan website.

At the interview

Be sure to arrive on time, preferably early so you can settle down and organize your notes, pens, voice recorder, note pad and other items relating to the task. In longer interviews (more than 20 minutes) the note pad is a mere back-up to the voice recorder, and you will be noting key phrases or points along the way. At the end, of course, you are going to have to transcribe the whole recording, and your guide notes indicate which bits are worth paying attention to.

You'll probably have half a dozen questions written down just to get things going, and you'll have checked that your pens are working and the voice recorder has enough battery power to last the session. It is rare that an interview such as this goes on for longer than an hour. Most magazine or newspaper interviews require no more than 40 minutes, and if agents had their way they'd be a lot shorter!

Remember your theme and the kind of things your reader will be keen to know, but always be prepared to change the thrust of your story should your subject reveal something extraordinary such as their becoming pregnant or announcing their sudden retirement.

After greeting your subject and getting the pleasantries out of the way, you should be spending 99 per cent of the allotted time listening. Talking about yourself, being overly chummy or acting like a cheeky television chat show host will minimize your chances of emerging with anything seriously interesting in your notebook.

The point is to allow *them* to talk, with you acting as the director of the conversation. Imagine they start talking about the sad death of their pet dog; this may be interesting enough to include in the article but at some point you have a duty to move the conversation forward. 'So, X, what about the new movie? Was it fun to make?' will do in this instance.

If meeting them somewhere special (their home or a fashionable new restaurant, for instance) be sure to observe your surroundings and take notes accordingly. Any interactions between them and others around them might also make it into the piece, so note down any suitable dialogue. This could be a joke with the waiter or a casual exchange with their housekeeper/partner/relative/manager etc. Being an all-round observer is the key here.

Writing it up

After the interview, you should have a lengthy tape script and a few pertinent notes and observations to take away with you. Now your job is to gather these together and turn them into a focused piece of profile writing.

Initially, you should look back at your notes and identify any key points and quotes that can be included. To be on the safe side, listen back to your recording in its entirety and add any quotes and observations that you might have missed.

It's not too late at this stage to continue your research, and there's no reason why you cannot contact your interviewee or their agent in order to clarify certain points. They, after all, also expect accuracy and by helping you, they are making themselves look good.

Indeed, celebrities and their agents increasingly demand to see the work of journalists before publication and can insist on their right for article approval.

From a serious journalist's point of view, this is not the ideal situation as what you should be aiming to achieve is a balanced impression based on your conversation, not an empty PR **puff** piece to satisfy the ego of the star in question.

In situations like these, it is best to gain their confidence by communicating well both before and after the interview and allowing them to help you get it right. This is in the interest of both sides and you may want to work with the same agent on other stories in the future.

What you don't want to end up with is a piece that has been entirely rewritten by its subject and stories like these do not belong in reputable publications.

By now, therefore, you should have four or five main points that you want to make about this person. In a standard magazine profile you will need to include:

- their thoughts on their most recent work and their career in general
- background, or how they became successful (where they were born, educated etc.)
- personal information (such as who they are married to, children etc.)
- their future personal or professional plans and projects
- your overall thoughts on them (they are brilliant, underrated, past their best etc.)

Intros

You must write an intriguing intro, either setting the scene of the meeting or making clear from the outset your angle on this person.

Here are some noteworthy examples, chosen because of their ability to encapsulate that person straight away and set out the mood or message of the piece to come:

> 'I'm not immoral, never have been. I'm amoral, that's different,' snaps Nicholas van Hoogstraten, a stickler for accuracy (at least his own version of it).
>
> (Profile of Nicholas van Hoogstraten by Jane Kelly, *Sunday Times*, 8 January 2006)

> Picture this. Every morning you wake up and have breakfast in bed. You read the tabloids, never the broadsheets, because they're too serious. When you're done with the papers, you get in the bath and watch cartoons ... This is how you start your day, every day. Then you remember you are not Richie Rich. You are not eight years old, you're 46 with an empire to run.
>
> (Profile of Simon Cowell by Ariel Leve, *Sunday Times*, 30 October 2005)

> On-screen she has brooding charisma, with smouldering eyes and fierce intensity. Her elegant, arched eyebrows suggest perfection, self-control and sexiness. She collected her Oscar for *The Constant Gardener* heavily pregnant with her fiancé director

> Darren Aronofsky's child: an image of achievement, capability and strength. It's an intimidating combination.
>
> (Profile of actress Rachel Weisz by Chrissy Iley, *Source* magazine, November 2007)

Using quotes

Quotes must be intelligently used, not just trowelled onto your copy to fill the gaps. Short, punchy quotes can be as effective as long, revealing ones, and even before the piece is laid out it's worth choosing some choice 'pull quotes' – those bold, snappy extracts designed to reel readers in.

You will need to edit their exact words if there are basic grammatical errors. 'We done 400 miles before the engine blew' should be changed, obviously, but there are instances in which a colloquial or foreign expression can add useful colour. As a rule, you should try to keep the quote's original flavour but don't overdo any nuances in speech.

Endings

A good ending is vital. Readers will want to know what conclusions you have reached after meeting your subject. Did X live up to your expectations? Was X intelligent/charming/vain/boring etc? Was your meeting a positive or a negative one?

Let's therefore contrast the above intro examples with their final paragraph:

> He likes the idea of himself in late middle age, dispensing advice to less experienced folk, a way of feeling good about power. 'People still come to me for advice. I am going to go on being a Samaritan,' he says. 'I've never intimidated anyone – well, have I?'
>
> (Profile of Nicholas van Hoogstraten, *Sunday Times*, 8 January 2006)

> Before he goes, one last question: what makes him laugh? He hesitates for half a second. 'Other people's misfortunes. Or being in serious meetings. Whatever is the inappropriate thing to do makes me laugh. When the worst thing you can do is laugh,

that's what makes me laugh.' He grins like a mischievous eight-year-old.

(Profile of Simon Cowell, *Sunday Times*, 30 October 2005)

Of the diverse characters she's played, she says, 'It's interesting to act people who are twisted. But in real life I like normal things, like to love and to be loved.'

(Profile of actress Rachel Weisz, *Source* magazine, November 2007)

ASK DAN

What goes wrong in interviews and how can I prevent them from happening to me?

If you have planned your interview sufficiently and enter the room with enough basic knowledge about your subject and an idea of what you want from them, there is no reason why it won't be a success. 'Fail to prepare, prepare to fail', as the maxim goes.

Interviews go wrong when journalists are rude and cocky or when the celebrity is tired or has a point to score against your publication.

Other nightmares include tape recorders that malfunction mid-way or recordings that turn out to be inaudible once back in the office. In the event, you must salvage what you can from your notes or go cap in hand to their agent and request a follow-up telephone interview.

Can I sell an exclusive celebrity interview to various publications?

If you have offered a publication an 'exclusive', then the publication owns the copyright to your words (more of this in Chapter 10). If you are a freelance, this does not prevent you from writing up a number of versions for different non-competing publications.

Say, for instance, you have interviewed a famous rock legend, the possible target markets include:

- music weeklies and monthlies (focusing on the new album or previous achievements)
- women's titles or female-focused newspapers (is there a family angle you could exploit?)
- English language titles overseas (assuming they have heard of your star over there)
- specialist lifestyle magazines (perhaps your star is a keen mountain climber or art collector)

Being a regular profile writer can pay handsome dividends financially, but there is a skill in being able to exploit your time with the rich and famous. Ideally, your publication is paying you sufficiently to accept a one-off payment, but you'd be amazed how many secondary and tertiary markets (including online, business and contract titles) exist.

Is it ever a good idea to write an unflattering profile?

The majority of publications, especially glossy lifestyle magazines and contract titles, will expect you to write an upbeat and complimentary piece. Editors and celebrity agents are keen to cultivate harmonious long-term working relationships and one bad write-up could have disastrous results.

Writers need to bear this in mind, and as agents are increasingly the main route to the stars, they must exercise a degree of respect. If you start to get a reputation as a harsh or controversial interviewer (alas, we can't all be Dorothy Parker or Hunter S. Thompson), the requests to do more will soon dry up.

6

Reporting the news

'You'll have to develop the habit of squeezing information out of the people I send you to see … and poke your nose in everywhere even when people slam the door in your face.'
From Bel-Ami *by Guy de Maupassant*

What makes an event newsworthy enough to grace the pages of newspaper, a website or a magazine?

In our fast-moving world, where yesterday's news is often a distant memory, there is no shortage of competition for page space. It is therefore essential for would-be reporters to grasp a sense of what makes a good news story before stepping outside to find one.

Let's start by considering the three events below and ask ourselves how newsworthy each one is. Are these the kind of stories that you would run yourself if you were a news editor?

1 The memoirs of a long-forgotten actress are published
2 A rare bird is sighted off the coast of Norfolk
3 The discovery of a cure for HIV/AIDS.

Okay, so we are missing a few vital details here, but if you are thinking straight away that it's the third event that deserves the front page treatment, then congratulations, you are on the right track. A cure for

HIV/AIDS would affect millions of people all over the world and even for those who are not affected directly, news of this breakthrough would be warmly welcomed.

Remember, news like this doesn't just affect individuals and their families or friends but also governments, scientists, social policy makers, healthcare workers, trend forecasters, insurers, urban planners, social workers, development agencies, undertakers, child adoption agencies and so on. Needless to say, this story is a biggie.

Yet this does not necessarily mean that the other items are unworthy of our attention. The ageing actress's memoirs could be hugely interesting to your readers, especially if she reveals some gossipy, celebrity-related incident. Let's say that she had had a love child with an equally famous star. Or that she had been spying for the Russians in the Cold War era. All of this is of maximum interest to your average passing reader, not to mention those who follow entertainment and celebrity weeklies or the political pages in broadsheets.

Birds, you might argue, are of interest purely to twitchers, and if you are the news editor of a respected publication aimed at bird enthusiasts you might be expected to run this story in your next issue. But what factors would make this story relevant to an even larger, more mainstream audience? If this species of bird is an indicator of extreme climate change or it's a Dodo, then tell your editor to hold that front page.

Most contemporary events, therefore, have the potential to become hot news items, the most crucial factors being that:

- something new or original has happened
- something has changed or moved on
- it affects the reader and their interests
- it is useful to that reader
- it needs to be published now

Where news comes from

With information becoming increasingly global, multi-formatted, and monopolized by big media organizations, it is not always easy to identify where 'the news' comes from.

Traditionally, news reporters rely on their hard-won contacts, and regular ring-rounds to them are expected to produce items of both local and national interest.

A reporter should also be aware of what's going on in all types of media. If you are working on a daily newspaper, that means reading all the national dailies as well as local papers and trade journals, plus foreign, ethnic and religious titles. You'll also be on the lookout for anything worth picking up from the latest consumer magazines, celebrity and corporate websites, blogs or Twitter pronouncements.

It is not unusual, for instance, for a national newspaper reporter to find big stories buried in the pages of say the *Catholic Herald*, *Motor Cycle News* or the *New Statesman*.

Right now, there has never been such a broad range of media available to journalists, and the trick for news gatherers is to find sources that work ou and to pursue story angles that are interesting, essential or useful your readers.

For a fashion news journalist that means reading piles of glossy, celebrity and trade magazines and knowing, on first name terms, all the leading industry PRs. An environmental reporter, meanwhile, might rely on poring over company reports or scouring in-house magazines and websites of relevant NGOs, charities and pressure groups.

Other than an impressively large contacts book and an awareness of what's going on in competing and non-competing media, the most reliable methods of generating a stream of regular news items include:

Press releases: Sent either to you directly or downloaded from an organization's website
Press conferences: Organizations such as the Metropolitan Police, the Ministry of Defence or Premiership football clubs use these to get their message across
Reports and surveys: Especially those focusing on health, education, lifestyle etc.
Profile interviews: Especially ones with celebrities already in the news
Being at the scene: You are the witness to a riot, earthquake, military *coup* etc.
Photographs: Supplied by a picture agency specializing in celebrity, sport, world news etc.
Ongoing investigations: When the findings of long-term research make front page reading, notably the 1972 Watergate scandal or the 2009 parliamentary expenses scandal
Organizational leaks: When an insider provides you with exclusive information that has news value
Tip-offs: When a member of the public has information of national or local interest.

As you gain experience as a news reporter, you will find that some of these methods work better than others. Above all, you should be prepared to update your contacts regularly and be open to new opportunities and experiences.

Say, for instance, you write for a drinks trade monthly and most of your stories come from company press releases. You barely have to leave the comfort of your desk. Yet there is nothing stopping you from widening the net and conducting your own surveys, meeting leading industry figures or campaigning for issues close to your readers' hearts.

How to write a basic news story

Having gathered all the facts and spoken to the appropriate people, you are left with several pages of notes which you must somehow transform into a razor-sharp piece of news writing that both informs and entertains.

The key elements contained in every news report are:

facts
quotes
background information

Or, if you are writing a longer, more in-depth report, you may have space to add:

analysis
description
comment

How you structure your story is entirely up to you and your editor, although the most important elements should always come first. Don't leave the juiciest bits until last.

In Chapter 4 we examined how to go about writing longer feature articles. Now we are concerned with pure news writing, which requires a more basic, stripped-down approach, free from padding and unnecessary comment or analysis. In the right hands, news writing is a fine art and there are some hard and fast rules to the genre:

1 Use plain English and avoid unnecessary words, repetition, clichés, jargon etc.
2 Keep sentences reasonably short

3 Use strong, active and evocative verbs
4 Avoid flowery descriptions or adjectives
5 Attribute all quotes (i.e. be clear who said what)
6 Use present or past tenses
7 Always be precise (i.e. 'About 1000 demonstrators', not 'plenty of demonstrators')
8 Avoid commenting yourself or putting yourself in the story
9 Use the correct names, job titles, titles etc.

Accuracy and objectivity are even more sought after in this game, and while you are still essentially writing about people and what happens to them, there is little room for personalization or in-depth insight – leave that to the profile writers and investigative reporters.

Writing a story intro

On the average news page, your readers simply want to know **what** happened, **where** and **when** it happened, **who** it happened to and, if you have the facts to hand, **how** it happened.

Here's an example:

> A woman aged 60 with 27 dogs in her car was pursued by police for 15 miles before she stopped, a court heard yesterday.
>
> Barbara Byrne – who had one of the animals in her lap – was also smoking a cigarette and holding a can of Coke between her legs as she veered across the A1 at 40mph.
>
> (*Daily Mirror*, 1 February 2003)

Analysis

Note the importance and effectiveness of numbers in this story intro (60 years old, 27 dogs, 15 miles) and how the woman driver Barbara Byrne is not identified until the second paragraph. This is called a 'delayed identification' intro.

Can you find any flowery adjectives or long, multi-syllable words here? Me neither. Note also the verbs used to record the events. 'Pursued' and 'veered' denote that there was no shortage of action while details such as the 'animals in her lap' and the 'Coke between her legs' only add to the story's quirky appeal and show that the reporter has researched it properly.

The story goes on to reveal that Mrs Byrne had earlier refused to stop for the police when they pulled up alongside her and that she possessed no driving licence which, combined with this misdemeanour, resulted in a year-long driving ban and a £125 fine.

In our story, this has been treated as mere background detail, the writer choosing to focus primarily on the fact that the woman had 27 dogs in the car, not that she was without a licence. Arguably, this is a more interesting point to make and it deserves to sit at the top of the story.

Notice also that the intro is a direct route into your story, and it outlines the key elements revealing *who, what where* and *when* before going into specific details. This is a standard method of beginning a news story and one that is especially popular in tabloid journalism.

Here are some other ways of writing news intros:

Summary: An Italian oil tanker laden with 3000 tons of diesel sank off the coast of Cornwall last night.
Question: Why did the Prime Minister cancel his appointment with 200 inner-city school kids?
Quote: 'Dear children,' says the first of Ofsted's new pupil-friendly reports published yesterday.
Comment: The new Employment secretary has only been in the hot seat a week but already she looks just the job to ensure bosses give youngsters a fair deal.
Narrative: There were red faces amongst Germany's police yesterday. First they allowed anti-capitalist demonstrators to enter the conference buildings …
Descriptive: Sobs shaking her slight frame, Linda Bowman could bear it no longer. On the pavement outside her home, the blonde-haired mother sank to her knees …

However you choose to start your story, the intro paragraph should act as the crucial first building block. Without a strong, accurate or balanced intro your story simply won't stand up.

So when reading back those first few lines ask yourself a few simple questions such as:

- Is this how you would tell the story to your news editor?
- Can a catchy headline be written from this?
- If published alone, does the intro still tell the story (without the details)?
- Would your first sentence attract a bored or distracted reader?
- Can you read your intro aloud without pausing for breath?
- Does your intro make sense?
- Are your sentences the right length (between 18 and 30 words)?

Structuring your story

Having written a brilliant and catchy intro, your job is to structure your story according to how much space there is to write it. Most news stories are between 300 and 400 words in length, but editors will often require one- or two-paragraph stories, the kind you see in the News In Brief section of a newspaper. Online publications expect reports to be especially snappy, with all unnecessary excess removed. On the other hand, newsy features, the kind you see in foreign news pages, can run to 800 words or more.

Be prepared for your story to be cut; news and sub-editors can be ruthless, especially when other more newsworthy stories such as a sudden fall in house prices or death of a royal family member take precedence. And if a hasty sub-editor needs to cut your piece from the bottom in order to make space, your words must still make sense and should be presented in a logical order.

For this reason, the bare bones of your story should be at the top. Your ensuing paragraphs deal with explanation (*how* it happened) and amplifying any points mentioned in the intro.

Analysis

A nine-paragraph story about an Australian surfer who survived an attack from a 16-foot shark immediately deals with:

1 The very latest development (a surfer who fought off a great white shark is recovering in hospital)

2 The background to the attack (he suffered cuts to his legs when he was attacked while surfing on Kangaroo Island, South Australia)
3 A quote from one of the paramedics in an Adelaide hospital ('... the shark just hit him from underneath ...')
4 A quote from Lee Francis of the South Australia ambulance service ('He is very lucky to be alive ...')
5 More background to the event (a spate of recent attacks has led to calls for a cull)
6 Further background (details of three recent attacks)
7 Recent developments in light of the attacks (the attacks have prompted the authorities in South Australia to provide a rescue helicopter that will patrol the coastline)
8 Statistics on shark attacks in Australia (there have been about 630 attacks in the past 200 years, about 190 of them fatal)

('Surfer fights off 16ft shark' by Maxine Frith, *Independent*, 26 September 2005)

Notice how the writer chooses to start with the most recent developments – the man is 'recovering in hospital' (present tense) not 'he was attacked' (past tense), and that subsequent paragraphs deal with separate and arguably less urgent points that explain how it happened.

The later fact that the authorities are providing a rescue helicopter might have also made a good intro but it lacks the drama and human angle of our brave and lucky surfer recovering in hospital. Perhaps for this reason, the writer has relegated this point to the bottom of the story, and if on a busy news day the sub-editor decides to cut the last six paragraphs, the story, and readers' understanding of it, is no worse off for it.

Checking your copy for accuracy

When you finish your story and are satisfied that any unusual spellings have been checked and all facts are correct and up to date, read through and see if it makes sense. Go back to your notes or confirm with your original sources if necessary.

Ask yourself whether there's anything you can do (including cutting or adding) to enhance the reader's understanding of it.

At this stage you should also be looking out for sentences that require changing for legal reasons. It's far better (and cheaper!) to change your wording now than attract the unwanted attention of libel lawyers.

One final point; news is fast-moving business with little time for reflection or analysis, and therefore your editor will expect you to turn your story around quickly.

Style types

As a rule, news story writers follow the standard news style – short sentences, active verbs, plain English etc. But style is dictated also by the publication they are writing for. There are a number of contrasting news writing styles in the media today. Here are the most popular:

Broadsheet newspaper or news website (sharp, concise, factual)
As a woman working in the almost exclusively male sector of engineering, Evans, 22, impressed the judges with her positive approach and her determination to beat industry stereotypes.

Tabloid (chatty, colloquial, opinionated)
As a woman in a man's world, plucky Gemma wowed the judges with the way she got stuck into her apprenticeship – not to mention the way she put two fingers up to sexism in the workplace!

Consumer magazine or mid-market newspaper (factual yet more personal and warm, sometimes championing)
As a woman forging a career in an almost exclusively male world, Gemma, 22, charmed the panel with her dedicated approach and the way in which she stood up to an industry in which women rarely figure.

Business to business (factual with a leaning towards jargon)
As a female working in engineering, Evans, 22, impressed the NAA panel with her positive approach to her year-long apprenticeship and her ability to overcome industry stereotypes.

How to use quotes properly

There is no excuse for a news reporter to get it wrong. Use either single or double quotation marks (check your publication's style first) and put full stops, commas and colons in the correct place. Here are some basic guidelines.

1 **If the speaker comes before the quote**: Survivor of the explosion Ben Adams said: 'We were sitting down watching the telly when there was this almighty noise.'
2 **If you open with the quote directly**: 'We were sitting down watching the telly when there was this almighty noise,' said Ben Adams, a survivor of the explosion.
3 **When the quote runs onto another paragraph**: Survivor of the explosion Ben Adams described the incident. 'We were sitting down watching the telly when there was this almighty noise. It sounded like there was a bomb going off.

   'At first I thought it was the boiler; there was smoke everywhere and all I could think about was how to get out.'
4 **When a partial quote is used instead of a full one**: Ben Adams was sitting down watching television when he said there was an 'almighty noise' in the flat.

Remember that any verb used by the speaker can be varied; *explained* or *told us* could easily replace *said* in this instance. Other popular reporting verbs include *claimed, commented, warned, added, replied* and *laughed.*

Code of Conduct

Members of the National Union of Journalists are expected to abide by the following professional principles:

A journalist:

1 At all times upholds and defends the principle of media freedom, the right of freedom of expression and the right of the public to be informed
2 Strives to ensure that information disseminated is honestly conveyed, accurate and fair

3 Does her/his utmost to correct harmful inaccuracies
4 Differentiates between fact and opinion
5 Obtains material by honest, straightforward and open means, with the exception of investigations that are both overwhelmingly in the public interest and which involve evidence that cannot be obtained by straightforward means
6 Does nothing to intrude into anybody's private life, grief or distress unless justified by overriding consideration of the public interest
7 Protects the identity of sources who supply information in confidence and material gathered in the course of her/his work
8 Resists threats or any other inducements to influence, distort or suppress information
9 Takes no unfair personal advantage of information gained in the course of her/his duties before the information is public knowledge
10 Produces no material likely to lead to hatred or discrimination on the grounds of a person's age, gender, race, colour, creed, legal status, disability, marital status, or sexual orientation
11 Does not by way of statement, voice or appearance endorse by advertisement any commercial product or service save for the promotion of her/his own work or of the medium by which she/he is employed
12 Avoids plagiarism

The NUJ believes a journalist has the right to refuse an assignment or be identified as the author of editorial that would break the letter or spirit of the code. The NUJ will fully support any journalist disciplined for asserting her/his right to act according to the code.

ASK DAN

Is it possible to be an ethical news reporter?

In the often adrenaline-fuelled quest for 'the story', it is easily forgotten that people's livelihoods and reputations can be ruined by the words that you print.

Doorstepping members of the public or revealing a source when they have specifically asked to be anonymous hardly count as the most sensitive of approaches but, unfortunately, they are common newsroom practice.

And such is the nature of the fast-moving and highly competitive environment of news reporting that, if you decline to pursue a story for ethical reasons, someone else almost certainly will.

That said, it is perfectly possible to report honestly and with integrity without compromising your job prospects. The NUJ's Code of Conduct (which all new members are expected to sign) sets out some basic moral guidelines and is a good starting point for anyone entering the occasionally murky world of journalism.

Is shorthand really necessary?

If your heart is set on less fast-paced reporting (i.e. writing opinion pieces or in-depth features for a monthly magazine), you might just get away without this basic journalistic skill.

Otherwise shorthand (Teeline is undoubtedly the simplest to learn) is worth having for all kinds of reporting, whether it's news, reviewing, celebrity profiles or feature writing.

In news reporting, speed is of the absolute essence, and with basic shorthand you'll be able to file your copy as less skilled journalists are listening back to lengthy tape scripts or trying to interpret the unintelligible squiggles on their notepad.

Learning shorthand doesn't take that long and your local college may offer evening courses. See www.hotcourses.com for details.

How important are press conferences as a way of gathering news?

Whether it's a major announcement by the US President or a product launch from a computer software company, being amongst the ranks of journalists at a prearranged press conference will ensure that your news organization doesn't miss out.

The trouble with press conferences, however, is that they are carefully controlled by the organization that holds them, and they never lead to an exclusive – there are far too many journalists present for that!

The way to view press conferences, therefore, is as a way of doing specific research or making better contacts in your field. Most press conferences have opportunities for both formal and informal questioning so if you are covering crime, for instance, that means the opportunity to get to know both police detectives and other crime reporters. These are the very people who will sustain your career, whether it's granting an exclusive interview or passing on the phone number of a well-known criminologist.

7

Specializing to survive

'From the moment I picked up your book until I laid it down, I was convulsed with laughter. Some day I intend reading it.'

From a book blurb written by Groucho Marx

Being able to adapt to change is one of the key skills required for long-term survival.

You may start out wanting to interview pop stars and actors for *Rolling Stone* or have your human rights exposé splashed all over the front pages of the *Guardian*, but you may have to settle (for the time being, at least) for a part-time sub-editor's post or a stint on a trade weekly.

Quality journalists rarely stand still in the profession and all kinds of opportunities present themselves if you are prepared to look hard enough.

This chapter therefore examines the more specialist areas of journalism such as arts reviewing, travel writing or sub-editing. Although they exist far from the screaming headlines of the front page, they have long provided writers with both a tidy living and a healthy public profile.

Most experienced journalists you meet will have gone down some, if not all, of these avenues in their career and you can bet that the fully paid-up foreign correspondent also submits travel pieces and book reviews for their publication; that is when they have a moment off from working on their latest television documentary or non-fiction synopsis.

Opinion columns

Opinion writing is one of the most highly sought after areas of journalism and it's a job that average workaday news hacks can only dream about.

If the salary isn't tempting enough (national newspapers pay upwards of £100,000 per annum for star columnists whilst magazine editors are known to fork out well over the magic 'pound per word') then imagine the freedom of writing about what you want without having to do the exhaustive ground work required for a news story or feature.

Unlike your colleagues in the news room or at the features desk, you'll be paid handsomely for your forthright opinions, not your fact-finding ability or knack of writing well-balanced copy. Think Julie Burchill sounding off about why we should go to war with Iraq or Jeremy Clarkson banging on about the Belgians. Indeed, this is one of the few areas of journalism where subjective opinion is actively sought.

Other than your precious views, editors will expect you to cultivate a relationship with your readers and develop an accessible and original style to back your ideas up. Look at any star column today and you'll find that most carry a picture byline which provides readers with an image or set of values that they can easily identify with.

For them, this makes a welcome contrast to the often dry, personality-free pages elsewhere and readers often gravitate to these pages first. Editors like opinion columns too because they appear regularly and can provide instant star quality. Controversial or much talked-about columns create welcome publicity and attract new advertisers and readers.

Opinion columns don't just have to be about politics or celebrities and there are columns for just about any lifestyle choice going, from single women to new dads and born again health fanatics. Who knows, maybe your next lifestyle choice will make for an interesting read?

Checklist: Opinion writing

1 Be informed

Column writing isn't just trotting out some of your old anecdotes and saying what you think about the world outside your door. To do this properly you must have a firm grip on all aspects of contemporary life from world news to politics, science, local government, celebrity gossip and sporting or artistic events. That means reading all the papers regularly, especially at the weekend. Reading is the route to many a worthwhile column idea and your readers will thank you for making the effort to do your homework on any given story subject.

2 Be controversial

Your views may have readers nodding in agreement or throwing away the page in disgust. Either way, your job is to get them to react. A dozen or more complaints to your editor is better than no reaction at all, and if you are putting the case forward for bringing back hanging by all means go ahead. Only do it convincingly and in your own inimitable style.

3 Relate to your readers

The best opinion columns are those that speak directly and with empathy to their readers. There's nothing like reading a comment you agree with that hasn't been voiced earlier and if this comes from someone you relate to, this is even more comforting. So if your readers are home-owning, Conservative-voting suburbanites then address the issues that matter to them. Equally, if they are a disenfranchized religious or ethnic minority then you must speak up for their rights.

4 Use your experiences as material

The editor is not just paying you for your skill with words but also values who you are and where you've come from. Everybody has at least five or six anecdotes that they reel out for the best occasions. Columnists store theirs (and other people's) like squirrels preparing for Autumn. Whether it's meeting a famous Hollywood A-lister or being robbed at knifepoint, your experiences will work themselves into your column soon enough. Change people's names if you feel that the telling of the story breaks confidentiality.

5 Have a style of your own

Having your own style of delivery helps to brand your column further and, hopefully, will make you stand out from the crowd. While taking heed of the house style of your publication, your writing can take practically any form. Is it best written in short snappy paragraphs or is it more measured, building slowly and surely to its argument? Perhaps it would work better in diary form (like Bridget Jones) or as a series of emails? Once you've got a style that works, stick to it.

Travel writing

For those who have a burning desire to see the world, write about it and get paid along the way, travel writing can provide thrills and adventures galore.

It is difficult to pigeonhole what travel writers do, where they go and how they go about their business; travel articles are written by both roving, free-spirited correspondents who ride donkeys and speak 12 foreign languages as well as desk-based editorial staff sent on pre-organized press trips by their editors.

Needless to say, the best quality writing comes from those who are prepared to go that little bit further or who are passionate about discovering new places and cultures. Such people invariably turn out to be freelances who have other interests and income sources outside journalism.

So if you are the kind of person who prefers a fortnight with your mates in Magaluf to sleeping alone in a Mongolian yurt, then this specialist area may not be for you. Travel writers usually travel alone (not with friends or family) so you have to be the kind of person who is happy in your own company for long periods of time.

Being well-organized and self-disciplined doesn't go amiss either, and as well as planning your own trips, which can be incredibly time-consuming and labour-intensive, you'll be handling your own expenses and chasing up unpaid fees. In the greater scheme of things, travel writers get paid poorly, especially if you consider the time and effort that is put into their work. And when you are getting paid by the word, not for your time (the standard newspaper rate is currently about £400 for 1000 words) the material rewards are nothing to write home about.

Having planned itineraries, haggled with airline PRs and eventually travelled, then you have to get down to the writing. Most travel articles focus on the writer's journey or final destination and in the trade these are called 'destination pieces'.

'Service pieces', the type that give readers factual travel information based on a theme, country or city, are increasingly popular, perhaps because they can be written up in-house by a staffer, and are therefore cheaper to produce. Service pieces offer top tips and practical advice and carry headings such as '10 Best Boutique Hotels ...' or '24 Hours in ...'.

Whether you lean towards the service style of writing or long to discover somewhere for yourself, you need to develop a knack of finding places and travel themes worth writing about.

And in a world where practically everyone can afford to take cheap flights regularly, you must have an ability to find new, original ways of writing about places in the world. You can't just ring up a travel editor and say 'I want to write about New York'. You must first find a convincing, topical reason for going (the opening of a major new exhibition space or the anniversary of 9/11 will do) and/or an unlikely new angle on the city. I once wrote a travel piece about my journey by bicycle from Manhattan to Coney Island – admittedly, not your average way of doing the Big Apple, especially as temperatures were in the mid-30s, but luckily an editor agreed that it would make a good read.

In a sidebar next to the piece, I mentioned other areas in New York that were suitable for cycling and supplied links to popular routes and contact details for local bicycle hire shops. It thereby gave readers an inspiring new approach to the city as well as practical service-style information that they could, if willing, act upon.

Checklist: Travel writing

1 Do enough research

The contents of your note book and daily travel log are the primary modes of research, so write copious notes on what you see, feel and hear around you, even during the journey there and back.

Otherwise, a voice recorder is handy for long interviews with local characters and a digital camera acts as a handy visual reminder even if you are not submitting photographs with the piece.

Before departure, be sure to contact the relevant tourist boards or organizations (such as the Red Cross or Youth Hostel Association) to help you find what you want and organize contacts or accommodation. Read up thoroughly on where you are going and look beyond travel websites and guidebooks. You might equally find inspiration in an obscure novel or film set there 50 years ago.

2 Stick to a theme

Whether part of a group press trip or travelling solo, it's absolutely vital that you have a strong theme in mind. You could be focusing on the food or music of the region you are visiting or comparing your destination to the way it was 10 years ago (i.e. before mass tourism). Either way, try not to end up with a bland overview, unless of course your editor has specified this!

3 Include people in your story

Travel writing isn't just about the places you have been to. It's also about the people who live and work there. As in any narrative story, characters bring life to your copy and they bring a welcome contrast to your observations and descriptions. Typical travel feature characters include waiters, barmen, taxi drivers and tour guides, but there's no reason why it can't be a fellow traveller.

When travelling alone, always listen out for snippets of dialogue that you can work into your piece. Two drinkers chewing things over in a bar or some old men arguing about football in the town square are all fair game.

4 Avoid the clichés of travel writing

Here's the rub. You are sent by your publication to an idyllic beach resort in the Philippines but how do you describe your surroundings without resorting to the clichéd copywriting normally seen in corporate travel brochures?

In real travel writing, 'dreamy sunsets' and 'virgin white sands' just won't wash, so you'll have to come up with some better descriptions of your own. The best way to avoid this type of thing is to concentrate on what you actually see. In your notes, list enough basic detail to make it yours: 'beached rowing boat with pile of rotting fish beside it ... two elderly women in black holding hands ...' etc.

5 Observe

Unless you are a well-known media face, your editor doesn't want to hear too much about what *you* got up to. By all means put yourself in the story – after all, it helps explain the premise of your article and pushes the narrative along – but don't overdo 'I ...' or 'We ...'

Your story should show that you are a keen observer and your finely tuned observations will help you to conclude your views on the particular place, activity or method of travel. Again, thorough note-taking and a willingness to go way beyond the routine tourist experience are key to this.

Remember too that you are providing readers with a kind of entertainment and they don't just want to hear how nice the pool was or that your soup was repeatedly cold.

Reviewing

Rather like travel writers, reviewers tend to work also in other areas of journalism or the media.

For those with special interests and passions, reviewing is a highly satisfying way of earning a crust. Think of the foodie who gets to eat out every other night and never picks up the tab, or the film buff who has advance copies of the latest releases arriving on his doorstep, not to mention the beauty writer who gets sent free make-up and cosmetics.

While many artists and performers remain sceptical about the value of reviews, they are without doubt a necessary part of the entertainment business. Without press or online reviews, the public may not know of the work's existence, never mind what it's about and where it takes place.

A well-written review is a piece of entertainment in its own right, and whether it praises or damns the work, it serves as valuable pre-publicity for the artist's PR machine.

Like news reports, reviews are written to specific word counts, and unless you are writing for the *London Review of Books* or the *Times Literary Supplement*, your copy should be short, sharp and straight to the point.

Don't be afraid to give bad reviews – these, in fact, are often the most entertaining kind for readers – but if you are going to make a name for yourself as a hard-hitting critic, be sure to know your subject inside out and back your opinions up convincingly.

And before going ahead with writing it, make sure you have the all the necessary facts to hand. That means reading the press pack or synopsis beforehand and swotting up on key protagonists/writers/directors/special effects people etc. and their previous work. Good reviewers are always able to put the work in context, for instance: 'How album X compares to this artist's last release' or 'This book is the best by writer Y for a decade'.

If you can prove that you are knowledgeable enough to claim a worthwhile opinion and write in a sassy, upbeat style suitable for print and online publications then you have a head start.

Getting into reviewing isn't easy and can be a bit of a closed shop. Reviews editors, after all, can pick and choose their contributors and will no doubt already have a committed roster of regular writers.

Start by choosing the obscurer artistic events, the kind that they would normally ignore, and tell them you want to review it. If they ask you to send it in, be sure to write it up in the house style of the intended publication. And if you are an architect and are covering an exhibition on house design, then say this in your proposal. Any supporting reasons for you doing the review (as opposed to their regular critic) are worth mentioning.

There's nothing stopping you also from sending in some sample reviews. It should be made clear that these are not intended for publication but to show you have the talent to be considered in the future.

If you are serious about being a restaurant or bar reviewer, for example, start contacting relevant PR companies to find out about future openings and launches. Get on their mailing list of friendly journalists. Indeed, the same principle applies to any type of reviewing, whether it's cars, comedy, television drama or health spas.

Checklist: Reviewing

1 Write for your audience

As a specialist yourself it is tempting to show off your knowledge of a subject, but it's the reader who should be uppermost in your mind. Ask yourself 'Will they understand this reference?' or 'Is this the sort of word they would use to describe this?'

Film reviews for *News of the World* and *Sight and Sound* (the specialist film title) vary dramatically in style. Readers of the former expect no-nonsense opinion with short punchy words and minimal background detail. Words like 'seminal' and '*auteur*' are likely to be a turn-off.

Sight and Sound readers, meanwhile, expect in-depth analysis and an understanding of cinema history as well as thoughts on the production or marketing process.

2 Make your opinions clear

Outline what you thought of the work, setting out clearly what was good or bad about it. Sitting on the fence by saying things like 'it wasn't bad in parts' or 'I quite liked the ending' just won't do – leave comments like that to the ordinary punters. You are now a journalist and must start thinking like one.

3 Provide background

Reviewers are rather like news reporters in that they are providing detailed factual information and sufficient background for the required length of piece.

For a film review, for instance, you'd be expected not only to find out who produced, directed and starred in it, but to summarize the plot briefly and quote directly from the screenplay, adding any interesting facts or anecdotes surrounding its making.

If, for example, you find out that the lead actor signed her contract on the back of a restaurant table napkin, then put this in; it's a good story.

4 Be accurate

Unless you are happy with the prospect of libel lawyers beating a path to your editor's door, be sure that you report accurately and professionally. That means spelling the lead's name right in a play or providing the right telephone number or dates for booking purposes. Restaurant reviewers must accurately quote names of dishes and their prices, and if the food is a disgrace, be sure to say precisely why.

5 Entertain

Naturally, you have a responsibility to say whether the object of your review is worth the reader's time or money. But when done well, reviews can be considered works of art in their own right.

Grab the reader straight away with a provocative or intriguing intro and don't let the reader go thereafter. In reality, they will probably never get round to enjoying this book/play/film/band/restaurant/computer game etc. but they've had fun both reading your entertaining and informative write-up and talking about it to their friends or colleagues.

Jane Cornwell on reviewing

Jane is a specialist music and arts reviewer for the *Evening Standard* and *Songlines* magazine.

How did you first get into reviewing?
Right place, right time. I was going to the Edinburgh Fringe Festival as a girlfriend of a comedian performing there, so I asked one of the major newspapers in Australia if I might write about the Australian contingent. I later met someone who knew a reviews editor, so I started writing about music.

What do you enjoy most about it? Are there any perks?
The free tickets are obviously a perk, as is the access to VIP areas.

What are the everyday challenges facing reviewers?
It is difficult to have to turn a piece around to deadline when you are dog-tired. I remember driving all the way back from a provincial festival to write a review that had to be filed that evening, and I sat there in front of a blank screen, panicking. I have got it down to a fine art now.

What skills do you need to be good reviewer?
Powers of description first and foremost. Also punchy copy that takes the reader there.

How important is it to get your opinion across?
Sometimes it's vital; you can't give a review two stars and not explain why. Other times you might be content with simple description.

If you really want to make a name for yourself you have to get your personality across, although not normally at the expense of whoever you are reviewing.

Is it easy to make a living from reviewing?
Not in the slightest.

What advice do you have for anyone hoping to get into reviewing today?
Specialize and be tenacious. Send in sample reviews to the magazine or newspaper or website you want to write for. Look at existing reviews, gauge the tone and word count. Write for free, just to get your byline out there.

Gossip and celebrity news

Most people working in journalism have an almost insatiable love of gossip and intrigue.

In recent years, celebrity chit chat has burst forth from the old diary pages and short news sections to the front page and beyond. Dozens of popular websites are dedicated to the coming and goings of the famous, no matter how trivial and, in some parts of the media, it is the celebrities and their agents who are setting the agenda.

Despite a rather crowded marketplace stuffed with agents, paparazzi and camera phone-wielding 'citizen journalists', there continue to be opportunities to catch some stardust and earn a decent living as a gossip writer.

Whether you follow the example of Popbitch or Perez Hilton and set yourself up on the web, or instead choose to uncover exclusives for the better paying tabloids, you need to get working on that contacts book.

There is no magic formula for uncovering the kind of story that will get the nation's pubs and staff canteens buzzing, but needless to say there is a certain amount of groundwork involved.

The top sources for gossip include:

- attending launches, film premieres, charity events etc

- photographs
- the internet, especially celebrity websites and Twitter feeds
- titbits from published interviews
- follow-ups from other sources (e.g. radio interview, magazine or local newspaper)

Remember: just because you hear something printable or read it on the page, it doesn't necessarily mean that it's true. There is a fine distinction between rumour and gossip and the journalist's job is to identify what is worth writing about and, once decided on this, to check that it's true.

Say, for instance, that you attend a film premiere and at the post-screening party you chat to the film's star who tells you over canapés that she is thinking of opening a new drama school in her home town. You note this down mentally – don't for heaven's sake tell your friends! – and follow this information up with her agent first thing the next day. Ask them: 'Is it true that X is financing a new drama school?' If the answer is yes, continue with: 'When is the project expected to be completed?', 'How much money is she donating to the foundation of it?' or 'Do you think your client would talk to me about this in more depth?' At this point, too, you will be underlining how positive you think this story will be and that the news will coincide nicely with the launch of her new movie.

Publishing scandalous stories without checking your facts could lead to an appearance in the High Court or an embarrassing out-of-court settlement. Celebrities are notorious for keeping their libel lawyers busy (and their lawyers' children in years of private education), so gossip writers have a responsibility to maintain their notes, tape scripts or photographic evidence.

If there are any sentences in your copy which you think might alert a keen libel lawyer (such as 'X can't sing to save his life' or 'Y is a drug addict') then make appropriate changes. It's far better to alter the meaning slightly than leave your editor with £1m in damages plus legal fees.

Sub-editing

Both an excellent way of getting your foot in the door of a publication, and a direct route to a steady if not remarkable income, sub-editing remains one of journalism's most sought-after specialist areas.

Unlike freelance writers, sub-editors, or 'subs', are paid day rates (up to £200 per day) and can work reasonably flexibly, which makes good financial sense for anyone looking for a way into the industry without the responsibility or pressures of a regular job.

Many established feature writers, editors and novelists have served time as sub-editors and there is a distinct long-term advantage of working alongside top editorial teams.

The sub is an essential part of that team, and their services are in constant demand, especially as a publication's press day looms.

Anyone thinking of a future as a sub-editor should first of all have a love of the English language and appreciation of its finer points. If you are the sort of person who can apply commas and colons effectively or frets over capital letters and the deployment of italics, subbing could be right up your street.

Working somewhere between editor and the art director, sub-editors must demonstrate a keen eye for detail and are responsible for a number of important areas of the production process. These include:

1 Checking that copy is written to the correct length and in the appropriate house style
2 Checking for accuracy, especially names, places, dates, numbers, prices etc.
3 Reading through the copy to ensure that it is intelligible, easy to read and appetising
4 Checking for libellous sentences
5 Writing appropriate headlines, standfirsts and picture captions

Clearly, if the copy in front of you already sparkles and the story is set out logically and there is nothing suspiciously wrong factually or numerically, the chances are that it will need only the slightest clean-up; perhaps a capital letter, a missing apostrophe or a telephone number check will do.

At times, however, copy that comes into your in-tray can require somewhat more attention, and in cases like these it should be returned back to the contributor for a rewrite. But when deadlines creep up or a page needs filling fast, it is invariably the sub who makes the crucial and final adjustments.

Generally speaking, longer articles are subbed on printed-up 'hard copy' and the sub's marks and recommendations are set out for the relevant section editor to read. Short articles (fewer than 500 words) can usually be subbed on screen.

Once all queries about the text have been answered (subs frequently end up ringing sources or checking information online) the copy can then be transferred onto the live page. It is here that the sub must supply a headline, a standfirst and, if necessary, a picture caption. This is arguably the best bit, and certain publications depend on the quality and wit of their headline writing.

In magazine layouts, subs have to scan the copy for a suitable pull quote – the kind that would make a casual reader sit up and take notice. Other than this, subs need to keep a sharp eye on every sentence or paragraph that passes in front of them, and if they are able to spot an uncapitalized trade name, a superfluous zero or even an entire hole in the story before the editor sees it, then their job is done.

Advertorials

Normally associated with upmarket glossy magazines, **advertorials** are pages that are paid for by advertisers then given an extra special treatment by an in-house copy writer and art director to make them really look part of the publication.

Writing these can be an interesting and financially rewarding sideline and clients range from travel companies and tourist boards to high street retailers and technology manufacturers. Depending on the advertiser's budget, fees can exceed those paid elsewhere.

Of course, advertorials don't count as 'real' journalism – the writer is far too busy serving his commercial master for that – yet similar disciplines to magazine feature writing come into play and writers must craft catchy headlines and intros and sell the product without making it obvious that it is essentially an advertisement.

Top tip: for those wishing to get into advertorial writing, try approaching the in-house departments of leading magazine publishers and show them examples of your work.

8

Online and beyond

'Things never stay the same. Either you learn to go with the flow and change as rapidly as you are able, or you will be left stranded.'

Felix Dennis, founder of Dennis Publishing

The demise of traditional print media has been predicted since the dawn of the internet back in the 1990s, and yet the majority of established publications continue to attract advertisers while registering surprisingly healthy sales figures.

What *has* changed during this time is the different ways readers access their essential everyday information, and whether it's a new recipe, a television programme listing, a sports score or the weather forecast, there are hundreds of other exciting new ways to find it.

Whether they like it or not, newspapers and magazines simply no longer have a monopoly on the latest news and opinions, and they must slug it out with competing television, radio, websites, blogs, podcasts or text messaging services. Indeed major news organizations take these developments so seriously that they have been prepared to invest heavily in new media, sometimes at the expense of their print version counterparts.

So with our mainstream media coming to such an important crossroads in its technological development, this leaves survival-conscious journalists with a tricky conundrum.

Do they join the digital bandwagon and retrain themselves in web production or video and sound recording or should they stick to old-fashioned reporting with its emphasis on hard-won facts and detailed research?

The answer is probably a bit of both. There really is no point in immersing yourself in new technology unless this can be allied to traditional journalistic skills such as news gathering or interviewing.

Leading news websites such as www.bbc.co.uk or www.guardian.co.uk continue to employ trained and experienced writers and editors and, right now, the quality of journalism on such sites is far from being compromised.

The message therefore is to embrace the new technology and be open to multi-tasking, and if you can offer potential employers a portfolio of skills you should be able to manoeuvre your way effortlessly through this exciting and innovative era.

Writing for online publications

The first thing to consider about writing for any online publication (OP) is how the reader is going to digest your words.

As opposed to a newspaper or magazine page which might be laid out on a breakfast table or lap during a train commute, online articles are read on screen, invariably at the workplace or on a shared home PC.

Most web pages already contain dozens of ads, banners, photos, film clips, soundbites and other distractions and therefore the copy itself does not have quite the authority of that found in a printed publication.

Writers, therefore, must be even more conscious of the short attention span of the reader, and use language accordingly. This means straightforward intros, short sentences and paragraphs (often no more than a sentence each) and little in the way of deep analysis, comment or background information. Like news stories which appear in print, quotes are vital although you must break these down so they fit into the snappy and succinct style of online reporting and the OP's house style.

The advantage of producing a news web page is that there are far more possibilities editorially. Whereas print publications have headlines, standfirsts, pictures and pull quotes, a web page can accommodate anything from an audio clip to a slide show. Then there's the extra bonus that the

UR BLOG
CONTACT
C.V
WEBSITE

page is essentially 'live' and therefore ideally suited to reporting breaking news and interactive content.

This obvious attraction means that newspapers, especially local papers carrying evening editions, have been especially hard hit. Readers and advertisers are deserting these once mighty community-driven publications in droves to get the latest up-to-the-second news elsewhere.

And if you consider major world events such as 9/11 or the 2008 Mumbai attacks, a web page is the ideal medium from which to show readers how continuous news events unfold.

Here are some key features of the average online news page along with their uses:

Audio clips: For recorded testimonies with key protagonists or witnesses via a press conference or on-the-spot interview
Film clips: For exclusive footage, interview or archive clip
Page updates: Copy can be fed straight onto the page as the story develops
Interactive content: Provides readers with the opportunity to respond to your story
Fact box: For presenting the very latest statistics on a subject
Map: To tell the reader where the story has taken place
Charts and time lines: Offer easily digested visual information and provide chronological background to the event
Pull quote: A key quote lifted from the main text and presented on the page in a larger, bolder font
Slideshows: Allowing readers to view multiple photographs of the event
Animation: Allows extra content to move on screen i.e. illustrations and charts

This is all very impressive, but as far as covering longer features and in-depth reports, web pages have yet to find a way of rivalling magazines and newspaper sections. Unless the reader prints the copy out on paper, dense text-based articles can be off-putting to follow on screen.

And for the moment, at least, magazine editors are safe in the knowledge that, as far as celebrity interviews go, nothing beats ultra-glossy pages and quality still photographs.

Simon Wright on online news writing

Simon is the deputy news editor for the daily news section of *The Economist's* website, www.economist.com.

What are your daily duties?

My day could include speedily writing an analytical piece on some breaking business news, or commissioning and editing pieces in-house or from **stringers**. Editing at *The Economist* is a bit different from other publications as we don't use sub-editors. So, as well as doing anything up to a complete rewrite of copy from a stringer less well-acquainted with our house style, I also provide headlines and rubrics, select pictures, organize charts, proof read and supply and all the other 'furniture' needed for a complete article. That said, the job is usually 10 a.m. to 6 p.m., though I work late and at weekends if need be.

What are the advantages of running a news website (as opposed to a printed news page)?

Pieces can be updated as news stories develop. And, in the rare circumstances where mistakes (literal or factual) are made, they can be fixed. Another advantage (which can sometimes make for a disadvantage) is that space is unconstrained so stories can run at any length.

What's the biggest difference that the web has made to news reporting?

A news website is expected to function 24 hours a day and is expected to react immediately to breaking news.

What are the drawbacks or limits (if any) of news websites?
The volume of news available has turned it into a commodity, which can discourage risky and expensive journalism. Pieces are often written as speedily as possible which provokes instant judgements rather than allowing the moments for reflection that some writers need to take.

How do you enable readers to interact?
All our articles have a link allowing readers to respond immediately and read other comments. We also run regular debates where readers can join in.

Do traditional journalistic principles still apply (e.g. short, punchy words and paragraphs, use of juicy quotes, balance etc.)?
There is absolutely no reason why they shouldn't.

What is the best way to get into business/web reporting?
You need to badger newspapers to let you work there (for free if necessary) and then make yourself indispensable.

What skills are needed to work and survive in an editorial team such as yours?
An eye both for the broad sweep and small details.

Using the web to your advantage

Far from being the threat that some journalists consider it to be, new technology has created a wealth of opportunities for creative types to market themselves effectively to a global audience and showcase their talents in a number of different mediums.

Indeed, survival-conscious journalists have no option but to adopt the latest new technology and find ways to boost both their profile and reputation in an increasingly competitive market.

That means joining online social networks, subscribing to news feeds, starting a blog or website and learning how to use a video camera professionally.

DIY websites

Building your own website, or getting someone else to do it for you, will not guarantee an immediate financial return, but it will allow you to share your best work with a ready-made readership (provided you publicize it properly) and perhaps one day catch the eye of talent-spotting editors and publishers.

For all journalists, having a professional web page provides a number of useful features, notably:

Biography: Write a few lines about yourself as an introduction. Keep it focused on your journalism as opposed to your other interests. Do not refer to family members or pets – this is your professional face only.

Text: As the copyright holder, you can share your latest published articles and archive them. If you specialize in several subjects, index them according to subject (technology, cars, gadget reviews etc.).

Blog: This is the part where you can really show off your writing and get things off your chest. Whether you are a political or social activist, celebrity follower or stay-at-home dad, there is a potentially large audience out there waiting for your next instalment.

While developing your writing online, bear in mind that it is your responsibility to find and develop a loyal reader base. This entails organizing time-consuming online networking campaigns. Without these, few readers will actually see your words.

Photographs: Why not enliven your page with a few choice shots? Obviously, there'll be a flattering one of you looking or behaving like a journalist and perhaps a few from your recent assignments. Photographer colleagues or friends should be happy to oblige.

Audio and video clips: How else are you going to display those recent television and radio appearances?

Links: Directing your users to your favourite organizations and online communities. Just ensure they direct their users to yours.
Contact details: So that the by now highly impressed editor can phone you on the mobile and brief you on your next assignment.

Emily Benet on blogging
Emily is a published author and writer of *Shop Girl Diaries* (Salt Publishing), www.emilybenet.blogspot.com.

What are the advantages of having a blogspot as opposed to a published piece?
A blogspot can act as a CV which instantly demonstrates your ability as a writer to a potentially massive audience and allows you to build up a portfolio of work.

How easy is it to set one up?
You need a computer, internet access and, for the best results, a theme and style that you can sustain over an extended period of time.

Do you need any particular skills?
One of the most popular blog sites, www.blogger.com is extremely user friendly. All you really need to know is how to navigate around the internet and the basic skills of a Word programme. You can preview any posts you write or changes you make to your blog settings. It's possible to edit and delete your work even if you've already gone ahead and published it.

It's helpful (but not essential) to have a basic understanding of **HTML** writing. For more IT-savvy bloggers, there are numerous widgets, gadgets and techniques that can be used in your blog to enhance the post content.

How do you get people to read it?
E-mail your blog link to everybody you know and everybody *they* know. Create a mailing list. Be open to social networks such as Facebook, MySpace and Twitter. Post your link on online forums (local community forums, writing forums etc.).

It's a good idea to claim your feeds in Bloglines and Technorati. Your blog will then be added to their databases, which will improve your search engine listings. It's also essential to add relevant 'keywords' before publishing an individual blogpost; this is called search engine optimization (SEO).

By adding a free monitoring tool such as Sitemeter, you'll be better able to monitor your 'blog traffic' and so can concentrate resources in areas that you know are likely to attract new readers.

How do you find time to write/manage it?
There is never enough time, but if you want your blog to be successful then you have to find it. Give up something else you do. Get up earlier. Write in your lunch break. Don't feel under pressure to write longer pieces if you can't keep it up. Write briefly and write regularly.

Is it possible to make money out of blogging?
Unless you can get advertisers who'll pay to appear on your site, making money from it is difficult. However, work can arise from a blog if you market yourself and attract the attention of people in the relevant industry. My book deal with Salt Publishing came about after I joined their Facebook group.

What drawbacks, if any, are there to blogging?
Blogging takes time and dedication. It's not always easy to come up with material every week, which can be frustrating.

What advice can you offer to those thinking of starting a blog?
You're more likely to attract a publisher if your blog has a definite theme or style. Images are always good and brighten a blog. If you write something when you're tired, let it breathe for a while before you post it online. Keep up a standard but don't be too precious. And when you're happy with your work, make sure you let everybody know about it.

Contract publishing

The contract publishing sector, also known as customer or corporate publishing, has witnessed impressive growth in the last few years, and existing publishers such as John Brown, Haymarket and Cedar Communications have been joined by dozens of new start-up companies geared towards producing magazines and other bespoke media for their clients.

A distinct sector from the almost exclusively sales-driven consumer magazines, custom titles are designed to meet the needs of specific brands or companies and act as a highly effective form of marketing. One of the most established examples of these titles is British Airways' *High Life* in-flight magazine. Other clients with high-profile customer magazines include Boots, M&S, Volvo and Amnesty International.

Indeed there are contract titles for all kinds of organizations ranging from shops and banks to hotels, charities, airlines and universities. In recent years, we have seen contract titles go international and magazines such as Ikea's is available in 10 different language versions.

The lifestyle magazine format remains a popular way of reinforcing brand or corporate messages, but contract publishers and their editorial teams also deliver websites, newsletters and direct marketing.

Here are some of the top contract publishers in the UK with a current list of clients.

John Brown: Orange, Virgin Group, Waitrose
Redwood: Boots, M&S, Land Rover
Cedar Communications: British Airways, Tesco, Central London Estate Agents
Haymarket: British Army, Manchester United, Jaguar

As the name implies, the success of contract titles depends on the relationship between the publisher and the marketing arm of the client organization. Publishers are offered limited contracts for the business, and when it expires, other publishers can make a pitch for it.

An important client such as an airline or high street retailer will inevitably bring in the biggest budgets, leaving editors in an even more enviable position than their consumer magazine counterparts.

Their long-term viability is measured not by sales (these are practically irrelevant) but by the effectiveness of the message conveyed to customers and the degree of strengthening to the brand.

Lots of experienced journalists from all kinds of backgrounds work in the contract publishing sector. If you have the ability to find new business and to offer your clients innovative and practical publishing solutions, it can be a highly satisfying and rewarding alternative to working for publications driven almost entirely by sales and advertising.

Mike Stanton on contract publishing

Mike is editor-in-chief of Canon Professional Network website and magazine produced by the Red Dot Agency on behalf of Canon Europe.

What are your everyday responsibilities?

I'm responsible for the delivery of editorial content on the CPN website and in CPN magazine, both of which are aimed at professional photographers.

I also set and monitor editorial budgets, consult on new projects and represent the editorial department at internal meetings and client and industry functions.

What makes editing a contract publication different from editing trade or consumer publications?

In many ways there is no difference at all. The techniques of gathering, editing and presenting content are much the same. However, contract editors act as consultants to clients as part of a company's communications strategy. In theory, clients know their customers - what they want, who they are, what they're buying, etc. - while editors know how to communicate information and ideas to them in a way that's journalistic.

How much editorial freedom do you have?

Total editorial freedom is a myth. Even trade and consumer editors work with restrictions, be it the political/industry stance of the publication, or those laid down by the publisher, or the pressures of advertisers. Put simply, in contract publishing the client is essentially the publisher and editor rolled into one, so they see everything, both in the planning stage and before it's published.

The freedom comes in debating the overall editorial strategy with the client and then choosing from the myriad ways it can be delivered.

Where do you see the future of contract publications?

The internet has radically changed the contract publishing landscape and made contract publishing one of the most dynamic areas of communication. Companies now realize they have to be publishers on top of their core business. Consumers, meanwhile, are no longer simply seen as 'targets', but rather as sophisticated customers who need to be informed, entertained, inspired and consulted.

Supermarkets are a prime example of businesses that know how to communicate with their customers and it's no coincidence that some of the best contract publications have come from this sector of business.

I therefore see contract or customer publishing growing, and content standards improving, as internet usage and sophistication grows. This also means more use of multimedia - many websites are now like mini TV stations.

How does an aspiring journalist find work in this sector?

There's no one route into contract publishing as there are so many types of businesses that want to publish a website or magazine these days. Being an expert in a particular business is one way in, starting off as a technical writer. I come from a mostly business journalism background with some consumer thrown in. This helped me to understand clients' businesses and the strategies they work to, and how to communicate them in a way that anyone can understand.

What skills are needed to work and survive in contract publishing?
Solid journalistic skills are important, as is a good knowledge of whatever industry sector you are publishing in. Clients like it when you know what's going on in their market, not just with their company. But there are other ingredients required for this kind of work, the main one being experience in client relations. This is where trade journalism or PR experience can be very useful.

What advice would you give to someone hoping to get into contract publishing today?
Look at what the biggest and best companies are asking their agencies to produce. Then check out the agencies themselves and what else they do. If you have relevant specialist knowledge never be afraid of suggesting ideas to editors. That's the kind of thing editors don't forget. And as companies are insisting on more and more multimedia on their sites, learn how to make short films or other audio-visual packages.

Trade publishing

Also known as business or B2B (business to business) titles, trade publications are produced for the readership of professionals of specific industries or trades.

In them, all editorial content (including the advertisements), relates to the industry in question and there is a distinct emphasis on providing useful information. One of the oldest trade publications is *Lloyd's List*, launched in 1734 to cater for those working in shipping and insurance.

Whether it's journalists, farmers, teachers, publicans or prison officers, all trades have their own newspaper or magazine.

Some of the best known examples of trade titles today include *Police Review* (read by police service professionals) and *Drapers*, which is the industry bible for people working in fashion. The journalist's trade weekly, by the way, is called the *Press Gazette* and in it are interviews with leading editors and publishers as well as tips from experienced professionals and pages of job advertisements.

Journalists working on trade titles must develop good contacts in their chosen field and show an excellent knowledge of specialized trades and industries. Here, the use of trade jargon is positively encouraged, although reporters must be able to communicate clearly and accurately. The livelihoods of their readers depend on it.

Finding that first job

There are no hard and fast rules to finding a job in journalism, but the most common ways of entering the industry include the following:

1 Work experience

If you are prepared to work hard without remuneration for weeks, or possibly months, finding a work placement is an invaluable hands-on experience which in some cases can lead to that vital first job offer.

It is advisable to choose a publication that interests you sufficiently for you to offer your services for free, and the right choice of publication can set you up with a lifetime of contacts.

Whether you are with a small local paper or popular consumer monthly, be sure you make yourself useful during your stay. That means picking up phones and offering to do the photocopying, as well as helping reporters with their research and, if you're really lucky, writing short pieces.

Editors remember people who can be trusted to do a job and when a junior vacancy comes up, the bright and willing work experience person is often highest on the list of candidates.

Remember, the smaller the publication you work for, the more responsibility you'll have, so don't turn your nose up at start-ups or low circulation titles.

If you can't find suitable work experience in the UK, try an overseas English language publication. There are hundreds of high-circulation titles all over the world aimed at working ex-pats, holidaymakers and property owners.

2 Applying for an editorial vacancy

By replying to a job advertisement, the candidate is claiming to have the required skills and experience to match the post. For anyone starting out in the profession, the formal application approach can therefore be a thankless task with the odds seemingly stacked against them.

This is where your self-promotional skills really come into play and much thought should go into your covering letter and accompanying CV.

List any experience or published pieces that may support your application and stress why, with clear evidence, you are the person to take on that position. If you have very little experience to offer, show that you are willing to learn and are prepared to take the publication further forward. Editors naturally respond to people with ambition and ideas beyond what goes on the page.

Show that you are the kind of person that they will enjoy working with and try to persuade them that they will benefit from your long-term input.

Jobs in journalism are advertised in publications like the *Guardian* (Monday's media section), the weekly *Press Gazette* or websites such as www.journalism.co.uk.

3 Bursaries, scholarships and in-house training schemes

Several leading news organizations including the *Guardian*, *The Times* and *Trinity Mirror* (publishers of the *Daily Mirror* and the *Daily Record*) offer in-house, on-the-job training. Places are limited, and due to high levels competition the application process is tough.

Elsewhere there are bursaries offered by the Scott Trust to study postgraduate diplomas in newspaper and online journalism.

4 Starting your own publication

This option can be extremely risky, especially at a time when advertisers are ruthlessly cutting back on their budgets.

But if you have an original and sustainable publishing idea (i.e. with a ready-made audience of readers), plus enough financial backing to take care of production costs, there is no reason to hold back.

There are dozens of independent publishing success stories to draw inspiration from and the most viable businesses end up being bought up by larger publishing groups, at great financial benefit to their creators.

Before starting any publication, make sure you have done enough market research. Ask yourself: 'Are there enough readers out there interested in this?' and 'Will they buy this regularly?' 'What will they want to read inside the publication?' or 'What kind of advertising and how much of it will I be able to attract?'

If you can find thousands of readers, guaranteed financial backing and committed advertisers you at least have a start. Now all you have to do is produce content – words, photographs, illustrations, design etc. If you can't do it yourself you will need to employ quality professionals to do it for you. Believe me, it is a big step, but that didn't put off the original editors of *Wallpaper**, *Playboy*, *Private Eye* or *The Face*.

Going it alone

'The only way to survive journalism is to do something other than journalism at least once a week.'

Channel 4 News presenter Jon Snow

Freelancing: it's no holiday

Taking the plunge and going freelance is a decision that is not to be taken lightly. To earn a proper living from freelance writing or editing requires enormous self-belief and the workload can make the average 9 to 5 job look like a relaxing summer holiday.

Unlike your friends or colleagues, who are safely ensconced in nice warm offices, freelances are always looking for that next paid job. Whether it's travelling to a launch party to meet useful contacts or surfing the web for interesting story ideas, the freelance's brain never stops ticking over and while your non-freelance friends have downed tools at the weekend, you are filing copy to meet deadlines or on the lookout for any leads or nuggets of information that might become your breakthrough front page **splash**.

Personally, I find that being a journalist (staff or freelance) helps sharpen the mind like no other occupation, and whether you see it as a blessing or a curse, nothing that you hear or see escapes from your trying to frame it into some kind of editorial context. The interesting person you meet at a party therefore becomes a potential magazine profile and the intriguing advert spotted on the train platform leads to an investigative piece. The exotically located book you are reading, meanwhile, is worked up into a travel article **pitch**.

That is the way it's going to be once you enter this world, so if you are the kind of person that simply wants to chill out in front of the telly and wait for the phone to ring, then please don't bother. Natural-born freelance journalists are proactive self-starters who have superb organizational skills and are unafraid of working long, unsociable hours.

And even with these qualities on board, success won't necessarily happen overnight, and there will most certainly be rejections and disappointments. The breakthroughs and interesting places and characters that you encounter along the way will keep you going, however, and if you stick at it and take advantage of any lucky breaks you get, you'll find that no other way of working compares.

Getting started

Headstrong ambition twinned with a mastery of language, general knowledge, current affairs, numbers and social skills are just some of the qualities needed to kickstart a career in freelance journalism.

But whether working from home or sharing an office space, freelances must equip themselves professionally before showing off their talent to the big wide world.

The items listed below will prove invaluable over a sustained freelance career and they needn't cost you the earth. Bear in mind also that media professionals must move with the times. When I first started out in the mid-1990s, I invested in a new fax machine and an electronic word processor. Although essential tools of the trade at the time, they soon became obsolete. Still, I'd like to think that my investment paid off.

Laptop computer

There are a few old hacks who persist with typewriters, but if you are going to start sending copy in to editors, the email with an attached Word document is the industry standard.

Desktop computers are adequately equipped for the job, but lack the portability and adaptability of laptops; when possible, journalists like to work as they go, and having a laptop handy means there's no 'dead time' before getting back to the office. Notebook-style laptops are especially suited to the job and they weigh a lot less, leaving you more space for other essentials in your work bag.

Printer

A working printer is essential for printing out your own articles at the editing stage or for filing as hard copy. Also useful for printing archive articles, web references or relevant press releases from **PR** companies.

Broadband internet connection

For research purposes and to negotiate commissions and file your copy to deadline, access to the internet is vital. To keep costs down, it may be possible to share your connection with colleagues or use public places equipped with Wi-Fi internet. Ultimately, it is a service worth having on tap in your designated workplace.

Telephone

Emails haven't replaced the need for journalists to make calls – far from it. A mobile phone is ideal for getting hold of editors, interviewees and PRs at all times of the day (and for them getting hold of you!) but when it comes to longer interviews or selling story ideas without any interference or background noise, you can't beat the landline sitting on top of your desk.

As a major business expense, the cost of your phone calls can be claimed back for tax purposes, so paying for an extra line, or sharing with another user, makes solid sense. If you make regular calls abroad, it's worth using a free online call service such as Skype.

Voice recorder

This gadget is worth having in case you don't have the advantage of shorthand, or if you are specializing in longer face-to-face or phone interviews. A digital voice recorder can, for a relatively small outlay, store all your conversations and allow you to listen back to interviews and select suitable quotes.

Desk space
Compared to other trades and professions, journalism requires relatively little equipment and few accessories. Your desk therefore doesn't have to cover acres of square feet, but it should be in a room where you can work without unnecessary distractions. Kitchen or bedside tables are recommended purely for short-term freelance work. If possible, try to create your ideal office in a spare room, ideally with quality office furniture and telecommunications.

Alternatively, try renting some real office space in an area of town that you want to work in or feel that there's an attractive buzz, with coffee shops and restaurants for luring editors, agents and PRs to. Rent and other office running costs are also tax deductible and there is a lot to be said about working in close proximity to others, especially if they can provide you with great contacts and stories.

Filing system

Everyone has their own approach to the storage of important papers and documents. If you manage them on your computer be sure to arrange them in easily identifiable files. Loose papers and hard copy should be kept in a filing cabinet. In this will be a file for invoices sent, payment receipts and expense claims, and there will also be space for relevant cuttings and printouts. Say, for instance, that you are researching an in-depth story about identity fraud. Every time you see a case mentioned in the press, you should cut out or print the article and file it for future use. Gradually you will build up files on all sorts of subjects, and in the long term these will serve as a highly valuable resource.

Stationery

A trip to the stationer's is unavoidable and you should stock up on reporter's note pads, invoice books and pens. A pocket-sized contacts book and one for your basic story ideas is also worth the investment.

If you are thinking of freelancing long term, it may be an idea to brand your business with some headed paper and business cards. You don't need anything fancy, just a smart enough design and font and your up-to-the minute contact details.

In time, you might also consider your own website with examples of your best articles or a page on a site showcasing journalists' work, but let those commissions roll in first.

Reference sources

Useful reference sources, such as encyclopaedias and contact listings, can increasingly be found on the internet. Nevertheless, there are a number of books and media guides still worth having to hand in your office, among them the annual *Writers' & Artists' Yearbook* or *Writers' Handbook*. Both list up-to-date editorial contacts for the leading publications in the UK and beyond.

If you are a travel writer, add guide books, travel literature, atlases and maps to the list. Film reviewers, meanwhile, rely heavily on film guides, biographies and great quotes anthologies.

The following are useful additions to anyone's reference library:

English dictionary (Oxford or Chambers)
Thesaurus
Events listings publications (on subscription)
Dictionary of quotations
Style guides (e.g. *The Economist* or *Times* style guide)
Anniversary and 'important dates' books
Brewer's Dictionary of Phrase and Fable
Business directories (e.g. Yellow Pages)

Or some useful references online:

www.britannica.org
www.oxfordreference.com
www.questia.com
www.bartelby.com
www.wikipedia.org

Transport

Maybe the area where you live and work has excellent public transport links, and therefore you can function without your own independent transport.

However a car, bicycle or motorbike is a great asset to the freelance, who must invariably travel at relatively short notice to cover stories.

Again, any outlay on running costs (including fuel) can be claimed as a valid business expense, so there's no need to suffer scoop-less on the top deck of a bus.

Bank account and overdraft allowance

Until the cheques start dropping on your door mat you will need sufficient financial support to get you through those difficult first months and years. Unless you have paid employment elsewhere or are sitting on a gold mine, it is advisable also to request a bank overdraft.

Even with the best intentions, publishers can be notorious late payers, and if I ever were to tot up the hours I had spent chasing unpaid invoices, it would run to weeks.

Passport

Just because you only report on UK crime or domestic football, it doesn't mean that overseas travel won't feature in your working life. And when you need to interview that ex-con in southern Spain or follow your giant-killing team to European cup competitions, there's simply no way there without a valid passport.

You wouldn't also want to be the freelance sub-editor who, when asked by their travel editor at short notice to go on a 10-day luxury safari, replied that their passport had sadly expired.

Tax advice

Unless you are a real whizz with the figures and are confident that your annual self-assessed tax return puts you in credit, then an honest tax adviser is advisable.

As a self-employed person, you must pay tax on any profit made (after expenses have been deducted) and file an annual tax return complete with your National Insurance contributions. Those earning in excess of £58,000 per annum are entitled to register for VAT.

For help see www.inlandrevenue.gov.uk/startingup.

Access to other media (television, radio, newspapers, internet etc.)

As your living will depend on your detailed knowledge of current affairs, be sure to subscribe to enough news and specialist publications or access regularly them online.

Listening to the radio, especially chat shows and documentary programmes, is a great way of finding interesting people and subjects to write about while information found online is increasingly useful, provided you can check your sources.

Unless you review television programmes, it's probably not a good idea to watch television as you work. That said, it pays to have more than a passing knowledge of what people are watching right now.

Expenses: what you can and can't claim

As you go from assignment to assignment, you'll begin to notice that the practice of journalism involves running up considerable personal expense. When not forking out on train fares, anti-virus software or printer ink cartridges, there are newspapers and magazines to buy, lunches with contacts and regular phone bills that would shock the average householder.

The good news is that as a registered self-employed individual, you are able to claim back much of this outlay provided it can be proved that expenses are 'wholly and exclusively' for carrying on and earning the profits of your business.

For the uninitiated, that means getting into the habit of keeping all receipts, whether for a bus ticket or a swanky new office chair, and filing them in a way that makes it straightforward enough when it comes to filling in the tax return at the end of the year.

In the quest for the next big story and the endless pitching that is often required to get it off the ground, doing your accounting and attending to other administrative affairs can quickly begin to take a back seat.

If possible, set aside at least half a day every month for checking that payments are up to date and for the right amount, and sort through and file any receipts that will later count as tax deductible.

The most common expenses that are normally allowed include:

Materials

Include in this the cost of a new computer, telephone installation or items of stationery as long as it has been used in the preparation of your work.

Your research may require you to buy books or rent DVDs or attend conferences. Expenses such as this also count as tax-deductible.

Premises

If renting office space, that means you can claim back whatever you pay your landlord. If working from home, a deduction for 'use of home' is normally allowed. This includes a proportional contribution to lighting, heating, maintenance, cleaning etc.

Motor and travel

Some expenses associated with running a car or bike can be claimed, including fuel and repair costs. Keep all motoring and travel receipts connected to your freelance work. This, alas, does not apply to holidays or leisure day trips.

Finance and administration

These apply to costs connected to the running of your business such as secretarial work or the preparation of a tax return by an accountant. What are *not* normally permitted as viable business expenses include:

- travel to and from your workplace
- payment of council tax
- the whole cost of running a house (including heating bills) if you work from home

For further details go to www.hmrc.gov.uk.

ASK DAN

Is it better to be a freelance or a paid-up member of staff?

On paper, being a salaried member of an editorial team is an infinitely better career choice both financially and security-wise.

Ready-made contacts and the opportunity to work for an established publication as well as paid holidays, a pension plan and the possibility of being promoted to the editor's chair are all part of the package.

If talented enough, junior editorial staff can be expected to rise quickly through the ranks and sub-editors and editorial assistants really do become editors over time.

It is little wonder therefore that few staffers relish the prospect of leaving their desk to join the massed ranks of freelances.

The average freelance must work extremely hard to keep up with the salaries of senior editorial staff and their annual income is a pure reflection of their output; if nothing of yours gets published, there is literally no money in the bank.

On the other hand, freelances are not restricted by the policies of their editors and publishers and are free to expand their portfolio of clients, whether that takes in part-time editing, feature writing, reviewing, broadcasting or book projects.

How much can I expect to earn a year as a freelance?

Because of the vast differences between the way freelances work, this is a hard one to answer, although the more successful (regular opinion writers, reviewers, profile writers etc.) would expect to earn in excess of £50,000. This of course fails to factor in other potential earnings via television, radio or PR work, consultancy and lecturing.

Starting out is without doubt the most insolvent period of a freelance's life and at this stage you are doing very well to earn as much as £20,000 from your writing alone.

How important is networking?

Other than your innate talent as a writer or editor, the strength of your contracts, plus your ability to add to them, it is what ultimately keeps you going in this business.

In every journalist's contacts book there should be a healthy smattering of editors as well as media professionals (writers, photographers, designers etc.), random specialists and experts, agents and PRs plus names of useful people in organizations that you have worked with, or aspire to work with.

When starting out it is especially important to show your face and tell people what you are doing; join as many societies, clubs or online networking organizations as you can and attend public lectures and meetings. You never know – someone out there could hand you that vital first break.

Is working from home recommended?

On the face of it, a home office makes great sense; there is no difficult journey in, or need to wear smart clothing and you can work the hours that suit your personal lifestyle. If you can avoid long sessions on social networking sites, daytime television and constant trips to the fridge, there should be no bar to a productive working life.

If, however, you are the sort that craves work gossip and regular water cooler conversations, the solitude and buzz-free atmosphere of working from home might soon be a turn-off. In this instance, stick to your day job or look for shared office space.

10

Going it alone II

People are always surprised when writers receive money, as if they don't have mortgages to pay.

Writer and reviewer Helen Dunmore

This chapter deals with the real nitty-gritty of freelance life. It's all very well developing a nose for a good story, becoming a whizz at networking or being able to turn around dozens of well-researched articles to deadline, but without a safe and solid method of doing business, a sustained career in journalism will be financially unviable.

From the moment you discover what you want to write about to the thrill of actually seeing your article in print, a number of important steps need to be taken first. Your ability to negotiate professionally and strike a fair deal for yourself will be severely tested by a publishing industry that is increasingly dismissive of the freelance's needs and rights.

Being regularly commissioned is obviously the first priority of anyone new to freelancing, and this will depend almost entirely on the strength of your ideas and your ability to place them in the right publications.

Once you have convinced an editor to run your suggested piece, you need to begin researching and writing it. But before beginning this process, make sure that both you and your commissioning editor are agreed on the following points.

The brief

Whether your commission has been agreed in person, over the phone or by email, you must be absolutely clear about what you are expected to deliver.

Depending on who you are dealing with and what kind of story you are writing, your brief could be one simple, short paragraph or a two-page document outlining each point you are supposed to make and contact details of each interviewee with suggested questions for each.

Either way, there should be no doubts about the angle you are taking on this and what information you are going to supply readers with. If you have agreed to add a fact box or extra first person interview, then don't fail to do this.

In the brief, it should also be clear which part or page of the publication it is destined for, how many words are required, the required format for your copy, and when you are expected to file the copy (your deadline).

If possible, try to push your commissioning editor to specify a precise publication date. This is not always possible as some editors like to stock-pile pieces and use them when they are left with a sudden space to fill.

However, if they do give you a date (the sooner the better for contributors) you at least have a guarantee that you will be paid your fee. Many publications have a system of only paying on publication and, sadly, it is not unknown for freelances to be chasing payments years after their original article was filed.

Fees

Most editors will offer a 'standard word rate' (e.g. £400 per 1000 words) but there's nothing stopping you from asking for more, especially if your piece requires a bit more time or groundwork to get it started.

In fact, most editors will expect the contributor to negotiate, especially if their work is a one-off contribution. Writers should know the real value of their work and set out their stall accordingly. For instance, there's a huge difference between compiling a 'top 10' list feature researched on the internet and an investigative piece involving undercover work and dozens of interviews and testimonies, and the final fee should reflect this.

Once agreed on this, make sure that the editor puts your fee in writing along with the brief. A **kill fee** equal to that of half the original fee should be paid in the event of the piece never appearing. In this instance, the editor responsible should be able to give a reason why your piece was a no-show.

Note that fees can also be paid for providing background information, tip-offs, quotes and expertise. Again, these have standard words rates but are negotiable.

Expenses

Just because you work on a freelance basis, it doesn't mean that you can't enjoy the benefits offered to staff reporters.

Expenses, therefore, are divided into two types:

1 Those that you incur as part of your business (e.g. the purchase of a computer) and claim back as tax-deductible.
2 Those that are incurred during the research and writing of a particular story (return train journey or library reader's pass) and charged to the publication.

At the commissioning stage, ask your editor if they are able to pay basic type 2) expenses, especially if there is some travelling involved or a long overseas phone call to make. In both cases, keep receipts and send them along with your invoice to the managing editor who will start to process them.

While you are entitled to some basic expenses, it is a good idea not to antagonize your publication's accounts department with overblown claims. Bar, restaurant and hotel bills are rarely paid by publications, especially in times of economic hardship, and should be negotiated directly with the establishment in question.

Restaurant reviewers, for instance, prearrange visits to new restaurants on the understanding that they will get free publicity. When the meal ends, no financial transaction needs to takes place.

For travel destination stories, the writer is expected to arrange complimentary flights, accommodation and any relevant excursions. Your travel editor might be happy to stump up £50 for minor travel expenses (covering travel to and from airports, short taxi rides etc.) but you will be expected to pay for your own meals and refreshments. All publications are run on strict budgets and if you think they are some kind of bottomless pit of funds, you are sorely mistaken.

Invoices

Once your copy has been received and approved by your editor, it is finally time to send them an invoice for your work and your expenses.

Invoices are not only an effective way of reminding them that you haven't yet been paid for your work, but provide you with an easy-to-follow record of which payments have or haven't been settled.

Although tiresome in the extreme, you will need to go through your invoices file regularly and chase appropriate editors and finance departments for unsettled payments.

In an ideal world, payments are made either on acceptance of the work or at the time of publication. If payment do not appear after four weeks of publication, it is advisable to contact the publisher's accounts department.

In cases where your publication doesn't have an invoice system set up, there is absolutely no harm in retaining your invoice so that you have accurate records to fall back on. Needless to say, publishers find numerous ways of allowing payments to go AWOL. A good tip here is to develop a good phone relationship with both the managing editor and a sympathetic person in accounts. Find out their names, and if you get to meet them at the annual office bash, make sure you buy them a drink!

On any standard invoice, the following details should be included:

- your name and contact details
- date sent
- invoice number
- the commissioning editor's name, title and business address
- details of copy supplied with total word count (e.g. Arctic Monkeys interview for the Culture section, 1200 words)
- expenses claimed (add itemized details and attach receipts)
- fee (as agreed)
- rights agreed (see Copyright matters p.134)
- agreed publication date
- your signature
- your bank details

Your business address
Contact details (including mobile phone, email, Skype, Twitter etc.)

Invoice no:	**Date:**
27	18 November 2010

To:	**For:**
The editor (full name) Sunday Times Culture section 1 Pennington St London E98 1ST	Arctic Monkeys interview 1200 words

Agreed publication date:	**Rights agreed:**
12 December 2010	UK only

Expenses:	**Fee:**
£29.50 (Return fare to Sheffield)	£750

Signed:	**Bank details:**

A standard invoice

Copyright matters

Freelances all over the world should have more than a passing interest in the laws surrounding copyright.

The payment of rights, after all, is a concept that was dreamt up and fought for by creative people like yourself. Without the ability to sell rights to different markets, freelance writers or artists would literally starve, or otherwise find themselves in boring clerical or manual jobs, ruing the fact that their art had virtually no commercial value. Fortunately, this sorry scenario has been averted by a series of copyright laws, the most recent being the 1988 Copyright Design and Patents Act.

Copyright law comes into its own when the creators of original material are able to benefit fully from their work's value and retain their intellectual property.

As with photographers and illustrators, the owner of the work is the author, not the publication, and when writers are contracted or commissioned to write a piece they are simply assigning their rights to a publication, not handing them over completely.

This system allows the writer the freedom to sell rights for individual pieces of work to all kinds of markets. Therefore having sold one editor First British Serial Rights (FSBR), there is nothing to stop you from selling rights overseas, online or for publication on a CD-ROM.

Let's say, for instance, that you have written an 800-word profile on Cate Blanchett for the British newspaper, the *Guardian*. You have negotiated a £1500 'first use' fee with them (well done!) but feel that the piece has mileage elsewhere. You therefore approach *Easy Living* magazine, a women's monthly, to whom you sell Second British Serial Rights for the piece.

Seeing that Ms Blanchett is also big in Australia (she was born there, after all) you then sell the same article to *The Age*, a leading Melbourne news organization. Technically, you are selling them First Australian Rights. Another non-competing title in Australia such as a fashion or film magazine would get Second Australian Rights and so on.

Having profited from these transactions with print media, you then consider who would interested in the online rights for this piece. Celebrity website www.heatworld.com are happy to pay for extracts of your interview (you offer them World Wide Web Reprint Rights) and so your fee continues to rise again. At this stage, you haven't even begun to consider syndication, republication or photocopying rights.

Fight for your rights

In an age when newspapers and magazines are increasingly geared to placing their content on the web and other non-print media, it may come as no surprise to hear that journalists are frequently asked to assign 'all rights' to their work.

By complying with such demands, the author loses control of both traditional and electronic media rights, while the said media group are free to sell their work to other publications without giving you a penny.

Clearly this is a sad state of affairs, and unsuspecting freelances should beware. The only proper response to this type of 'rights grab' is to refuse to sign any document, including a commissioning brief, that waives all your rights. Instead, try to negotiate with your editor the various different rights or extra uses offered.

Furthermore, any article that is handed over with 'all rights' assigned should be worth more than four times the fee for a normal licence. That way, at least, you cover yourself from the anticipated loss in revenue suffered by your chosen media organization profiting from it themselves.

'Moral rights' are your rights to a byline credit, and to object if your work has been distorted in any way. These are equally important to retain, as they will protect you and your reputation from being damaged by poor editorial decisions.

5 things you should know about copyright

1. Staff writers do not retain the rights to their work. This is automatically owned by their employer/publishing company.
2. Story ideas and angles are not protected under copyright law, and therefore must be handled with care. Don't give away your best story ideas to unscrupulous editors as they will steal them.
3. You cannot own the copyright to headlines, single words and short phrases. Bad news for the minds behind '9/11', 'Metrosexual' or 'Gotcha!'

4 If using someone else's words in a piece of writing (such as a biographical extract or part of a screenplay) be sure to quote less than 'a substantial part' of the work. Officially, this is interpreted as a short paragraph or four lines from a 32-line poem.
5 Copyright lasts for 70 years after your death. You can assign copyright to other individuals or organizations, such as charities.

For more information on copyright see www.britishcopyright.org.

ASK DAN

What do I do if my commissioned piece gets rejected?

There are many reasons why pieces get rejected and it shouldn't always be taken personally. Editorial changes take place beyond the control of contributors and stories can simply date, leaving them redundant in a news context.

If you accept a 'kill fee', you are agreeing not to publish elsewhere. That does not stop you, however, from refocusing the angle of your story (as opposed to offering the same work) and looking for another publication in which to place it. After all, you have spent enough time and effort on meeting your deadline and it would be bad business not to.

The knack of freelance journalism is being able to find different markets for your stories and stay up-to-date with the latest launches or shifts in the media landscape. In theory, at least, there is always a home for a rejected story.

How do I establish the copyright for my piece?

Fortunately, this is a straightforward affair which doesn't require a lawyer and the signing of piles of legal papers. If your full name and the date is at the top of the page and you have written 'ENDS' at the bottom of the piece, you are the owner of the copyright. Simple as that.

Your task thereafter is to control the use of your copyright and assign it accordingly.

Do journalists get paid for their photos if they are published alongside their piece?

Freelances can boost their earnings considerably by having their photographs published alongside their writing. This applies particularly in travel writing or reportage where the journalist is working independently in remote areas or is continually on the move. In all cases, the photographs must be of an acceptable standard for publication.

Fees must be negotiated with the publication's picture editor, not the features editor.

By and large, publications prefer to use their own photographers and, once convinced that your story needs pictures, will send one to the appropriate event/location. For in-depth features, writers must brief photographers beforehand so that they understand what the story is about and who the most important people in it are.

•●● What can you do if your contributor's fee remains unpaid and your publication goes out of business?

Sadly, this is an all too common scenario and one which rarely ends with a satisfactory outcome. Freelance journalists are pretty low down on the list of a publisher's priorities, and when their business folds they will have prior loyalty to staff members. Remember, they too will be out of pocket and will face pay cuts or redundancy.

This is not to say that your case for payment of fees and expenses is lost. With proper representation (the NUJ offers members free legal assistance) the fees, or part of the fee, should eventually be settled.

The lesson from all this of course is to work for established publications with a good track record for looking after freelance contributors.

Useful contacts

Readers

Audit Bureau of Circulations, www.abc.org.uk
National Readership Survey, www.nrs.co.uk

Research

British Newspaper Library, www.bl.uk
Central Office of Information, www.coi.gov.uk
The National Archives, www.nationalarchives.gov.uk
UK National Statistics, www.statistics.gov.uk

Professional organizations

National Union of Journalists, www.nuj.org.uk
Chartered Institute of Journalists, www.cioj.co.uk

News agencies

Press Association, www.pressassociation.com
Reuters, www.uk.reuters.com

Media guides

Writers' & Artists' Yearbook (A&C Black)
The Writer's Handbook (Macmillan)
Media 08: The Essential Guide to the Changing Media Landscape, Janine Gibson (Guardian Books)

Resources for freelances
www.pressgazette.co.uk
www.journalism.co.uk
www.holdthefrontpage.co.uk

Blog site building
www.blog.com
www.blogger.com

Training and learning
BBC Training and Development, www.bbctraining.com
National Council for the Training of Journalists (NCTJ), www.nctj.com
Periodicals Training Council, www.ppa.co.uk

Undergraduate courses
University of Bournemouth, Poole, www.bournemouth.ac.uk
Cardiff University, www.cardiff.ac.uk
City University, London, www.city.ac.uk

Harlow College, www.harlow-college.ac.uk
London College of Communication, www.lcc.arts.ac.uk
University of Sheffield, www.shef.ac.uk
Southampton Solent University, www.solent.ac.uk
University of Westminster, www.wmin.ac.uk

Postgraduate courses

University College Falmouth, www.falmouth.ac.uk
Highbury College, Portsmouth, www.highbury.ac.uk
University of Leeds, Trinity All Saints, www.leedstrinity.ac.uk
University of London, Birkbeck, www.birkbeck.ac.uk

Production

InDesign and Dreamweaver, www.adobe.com
QuarkXpress, www.quark.com

Web design

www.2createawebsite.com
www.build-your-website.co.uk
www.350.com
www.moonfruit.com

Glossary of terms

ABC: Audit Bureau of Circulation
Advertorial: feature page paid for by an advertiser
Angle: the writer's approach to the story
Bleed: when a page or cover design extends to the edge or over the paper
Blogging: writing opinions directly online
Body copy: the main text belonging to a story
Broadsheet: large format newspapers denoting quality (*The Times*, *Guardian* etc.)
Byline: journalist's name attributed to their article
Caps: capital letters
Catchline/catch: catchy name given to a story typed on every page of copy
Circulation: amount of readers who buy the publication (weekly, monthly etc.)
Clippings or **cuts**: previous published work of a journalist
Copy: text or words that make up a story
Deadline: date or time by which copy must be filed
Doorstepping: when a reporter waits outside the home of someone in the news
DPS: double page spread
Drop cap: first letter of a story set in large type by page designer
Editorial: article that shows the opinion of a publication
FBSR: First British Serial Rights
Feature: story that goes beyond the basic facts, often with a strong human interest
Follow-up: story offered by a writer following the acceptance of a previous story
Flatplan: editor's page-by-page plan of a forthcoming issue
Gutter: space between the pages in a centre spread
Hack: derogatory term for a journalist
Headline: Catchy words or phrase written above the story
House style: the accepted style of a publication including rules on punctuation, numbers, official titles etc.

How to (story): article on practical issues such as gardening, personal finance or photography
HTML: Mark-up language used in web design that helps to structure documents
InDesign: popular page design programme used by magazines
Intro: lead-in to the story, usually the first paragraph
Kill fee: fee paid to a freelance to drop a previously scheduled story
Layout: the combination of text, headlines, pictures and captions on a page
Lead: information given to a journalist that leads to a story
Lower case: non-capitalized letters of a word
Masthead: list of staff and contributors found near the front of a magazine
MS: manuscript
NIB: News in Brief story
Off-diary: story set up by a reporter, not their editor
Off-the-record: comments that a journalist agrees not to print
On spec: story submitted without prior arrangement
Par: paragraph
Peg: reason for printing a story
Piece: written article
Pitch: story outline sent to a commissioning editor
PR: public relations
Proof: unchecked version of copy
Puff: insubstantial story that reads like an advertisement
Pull quote: choice quote made large on the page
Q&A: Question and Answer interview
Quote: the actual words of someone in the story
Readership: people who read the publication regularly
Run-on: copy that continues onto another page
Running story: ever-developing story that runs over several editions
Scoop: exclusive story
Sidebar or **box out**: extra information, such as key statistics, that accompany a story
Spike: to reject a story
Splash: lead story in a popular newspaper
Spoiler: story which is run to spoil a rival's exclusive
Spread: article or images spread over two or more pages
Standfirst (or **sell**): lead-in line before the main feature copy starts
Strapline: wording that serves as a page's heading

Stringer: freelance reporter contracted to a news organization
Sub: sub-editor
Tabloid: popular newspaper in smaller page format (*The Sun*, *The Mirror* etc.)
Tapescript: taped recording of an interview
Think piece: an analytical piece written to provoke readers
Tip-off: information given by member of the public
TOT: Triumph over Tragedy story, usually seen in women's weeklies
Typo: typographical error
Upper case: capital letters
Vox pop: interviews on a specific subject with random people in the street

Recommended reading

On journalism

Evans, H. and Crawford, G. (2000) *Essential English: For Journalists, Editors and Writers*. London: Pimlico.

The Economist (2001) *The Economist Style Guide*. London: Economist Books.

Waterhouse, K. (1993) *Waterhouse on Newspaper Style*. London: Viking.

News writing

Frost, C. (2002) *Reporting for Journalists*. London: Routledge.

McKane, A. (2006) *News Writing*. London: Sage Publications Ltd.

Interviewing

Barber, L. (1999) *Demon Barber*. London: Penguin.

Cooke, A. (2008) *Six Men*. London: Penguin.

Reportage

Davies, N. (2009) *Flat Earth News*. London: Vintage.

Jack, I. (2001) *The Crash That Stopped Britain*. London: Granta Books.

Klein, N. (2001) *No Logo*. London: Flamingo.

LeDuff, C. (2004) *Work and Other Sins: Life in New York City and Thereabouts*. London: Penguin.

Orwell, G. (2001) *Down and Out in Paris and London*. London: Penguin Modern Classics.

Pilger, J. (1998) *Hidden Agendas*. London: Vintage.

Ronson, J. (2001) *Them: Adventures with Extremists*. London: Picador.

Schlosser, E. (2002) *Fast Food Nation*. London: Penguin.

Thompson, Hunter S. (2003) *Hell's Angels*. London: Penguin Modern Classics.

Wolfe, T. (1989) *The Electric Kool-aid Acid Test*. London: Black Swan.

Biographical

Cameron, J. (2006) *Point of Departure*. London: Granta Books.

Young, T. (2002) *How to Lose Friends and Alienate People*. London: Abacus.

Frith, M. (2009) *The Celeb Diaries: The Sensational Inside Story of the Celebrity Decade*. London: Ebury Press.

Harris, P. (2009) *More Thrills Than Skills: Adventures in Journalism, War and Terrorism*. London: Kennedy and Boyd.

Hastings, M. (2003) *Editor: An Inside Story of Newspapers*. London: Pan Books.

Morgan, P. (2005) *The Insider: The Private Diaries of a Scandalous Decade*. London: Ebury Press.

Columnists and reviews

Brooker, C. (2004) *Screen Burn*. London: Faber and Faber.

Burchill, J. (2001) *The Guardian Columns*. London: Gollancz.

O'Farrell, J. (2002) *Global Village Idiot*. London: Black Swan.

Silvester, C. (1997) *Penguin Book of Columnists*. London: Viking.

Travel writing

Bryson, B. (1996) *Notes from a Small Island*. London: Black Swan.

Morris, J. (2004) *A Writer's World: Travels 1950–2000*. London: Faber and Faber.

O'Rourke, P.J. (2002) *Holidays in Hell*. London: Picador.

Collected journalism

Deedes, B. (2007) *Words and Deedes: Selected Journalism 1931–2006*. London: Pan.

Bangs, K. (1996) *Psychotic Reactions and Carburetor Dung*. London: Serpent's Tail.

Mills, E. with Cochrane, K. (2005) *Cupcakes and Kalashnikovs: 100 Years of the Best Journalism by Women*. London: Constable.

Index